Money

Síreacht: Longings for Another Ireland is a series of short, topical and provocative texts on controversial issues in contemporary Ireland.

Contributors to the *Síreacht* series come from diverse backgrounds and perspectives but share a commitment to the exposition of what may often be disparaged as utopian ideas, minority perspectives on society, polity and environment, or critiques of received wisdom. Associated with the phrase *ceól sírechtach síde* found in Irish medieval poetry, *síreacht* refers to yearnings such as those evoked by the music of the *aos sí*, the supernatural people of Irish mythology. As the title for this series, we use it to signify longings for and imaginings of a better world in the spirit of the World Social Forums that 'another world is possible'. At the heart of the mythology of the *sí* is the belief that laying beneath this world is the other world. So too these texts address the urgent challenge to imagine potential new societies and relationships, but also to recognise the seeds of these other worlds in what already exists.

Other published titles in the series are

Freedom? by Two Fuse
Public Sphere by Harry Browne
Commemoration by Heather Laird

The editors of the series, Órla O'Donovan, Fiona Dukelow and Rosie Meade, School of Applied Social Studies, University College Cork, welcome suggestions or proposals for consideration as future titles in the series. Please see http://sireacht.ie/ for more information.

Money

CONOR McCABE

Series Editors:
Órla O'Donovan, Fiona Dukelow and Rosie Meade

CORK UNIVERSITY PRESS

First published in 2018 by
Cork University Press
Youngline Industrial Estate
Pouladuff Road, Togher
Cork T12 HT6V, Ireland

British Library Cataloguing in Publication Data
A CIP catalogue record for this book is available from the British
Library.

ISBN- 978-1-78205-282-1

Typeset by Studio 10 Design
Printed by HussarBooks

CONTENTS

Introduction

On 19 November 2010 the president of the European Central Bank (ECB), Jean-Claude Trichet, issued an ultimatum to the Irish government. He said that unless Ireland applied at once for financial support from the Eurogroup (the other countries of the Eurozone) the bank would withdraw all emergency funding from the state's financial sector. Such a move would have forced a funding crisis, making Irish banks insolvent, with the country not far behind. The government had given a €400 billion guarantee to the banks two years previously but was in no position to make good on the promise. It was in a severely compromised situation and Trichet used it not only to force Ireland into a bailout, but also to insist that it commit itself to 'fiscal consolidation, structural reforms and financial sector restructuring in agreement with the European Commission, the International Monetary Fund and the ECB'.[1] The government capitulated and entered into a three-year Troika[2] programme with serious social and economic consequences.

The naked threats of the ECB, the use of its money-line as a bludgeon for its own political and economic purposes, are a far cry from the standard definition of money as an asset that simply functions as a store of value, a unit of account, and a medium of exchange.[3] This benign reading of money does not fit too well with the evidence we have of it being used to cajole and bully entire peoples into political and economic decisions that are clearly against their collective interests.

The price that Greece paid to stay as part of the euro was the decimation of its social supports through the implementation of the Troika's austerity measures. 'It is impossible to overlook the fact,' wrote the International Federation of Human Rights in 2014, 'that what started as an economic and financial breakdown has turned into an unprecedented assault on human rights and democratic standards in Greece and all countries sharing a similar fate.'[4] The authors said that 'limitations on human rights have increasingly been imposed and economic constraints evoked as cause for further restrictions' and as a result 'the founding principles of democracy, and the European project that builds on them, are dangerously and irretrievably at stake'.[5]

The imposition of austerity across Europe was justified by the argument that countries needed to be fiscally 'prudent' in order to have access to international credit lines. In reality, austerity was a scramble to save the international monetary system from its own internal failures. It was used to shore up distributional inequalities within the system rather than tackling the actual cause of the crisis which stemmed from 'an unsustainable and flawed neo-liberal model of growth and development',[6] one that prioritised free markets and finance over the public interest. Austerity was an act of self-preservation by financial institutions that was implemented with zeal by central banks, politicians and bureaucrats. It amounted to a direct attack on the lives of hundreds of millions of people.

Money, it seems, is hardly a neutral space. The financial system works for those who wield the most influence over it.

In Ireland's case, while the Troika bailout was foisted upon the state, the chain of events that led to it was of its own making. The decision in 2008 to give an almost blanket guarantee to six banks in Ireland – despite the severe problems that were known in relation to at least two of them, Irish Nationwide Building Society and Anglo Irish Bank – was itself a bailout of local financial institutions and a cohort of their property-based clients. It was an exercise in genuine political and economic power, one that put certain vested interests over the well-being of the state.[7] It was an unconscionable act that was not repeated in scale by any other country within the Eurozone. As for the banks, however, it was nothing more than what they, with their heightened sense of entitlement, expected at the time.

Five days after the announcement of the Irish bank guarantee, Seán FitzPatrick, the chairman of Anglo Irish Bank, gave an address at the annual La Touche Legacy seminar in Greystones, County Wicklow, where he called for the 'sacred cows' of Irish society to be tackled once and for all. These were, in his opinion, universal child benefit, state pensions and medical cards for those over seventy. He also called for Ireland's corporation tax rate to be cut to 10 per cent.[8] The cost of guaranteeing Anglo Irish Bank would eventually come to around €30 billion, around half of the total bailout funds sourced from the Troika. The legacy debt of Anglo Irish Bank will be on the shoulders of the Irish people until 2054. It is certainly true that Ireland has sacred cows, and in 2008 they were the ones given a blanket guarantee to cover their disastrous investment plans while they waxed lyrical about child benefit and medical cards when the mood suited them.

The bank guarantee was a solo run by the Irish government. The state had not consulted its European partners on the measure, informing them only when it was a fait accompli. It was 'a tendency towards economic nationalism and I regret that', said the Minister for Finance, Brian Lenihan, 'but we are on our own here in Ireland and the government has to act in the interests of the Irish people'.[9] He added that while it is important for Europe to protect its financial system, 'in the absence of a Europe-wide system there is an onus on the Irish government as the sovereign body with responsibility in this state to take action'. The unilateral decision by Ireland to give such a wide-ranging guarantee was one that other governments in the EU saw 'as a beggar-thy-neighbour policy'.[10] It was also seen as extremely reckless. The UCD-based academic Morgan Kelly wrote that the Finance Minister was 'faced with a choice between rescuing two banks and the handful of developers through whom they placed real estate bets or recapitalising the financial infrastructure on which the other four million of us depend. He chose the former.'[11] It is not unreasonable to conclude that a tiny but powerful section of Irish society did everything it could to protect itself, even if that meant the financial collapse of the state.[12]

'Real elites only enter the day-to-day operations of government in periods of crisis,' wrote William K. Tabb in his seminal work on the 1970s' New York fiscal crisis. 'They move to the background as soon as possible, after they have restructured the context of decision-making in ways they find congenial.'[13] Ireland during the 2008 financial crisis was no different. There was a rupture in the mechanisms and institutions that support economic class power in Ireland, and the political and economic strategy was to protect and rebuild those structures by whatever means necessary, regardless of the social cost. The nature of the crisis was such that some members of that class lost out – collateral damage, if you will – but the core remained, and the system was secured, albeit tentatively. This was done via an unprecedented transfer of collective wealth from the citizenry to the banking system, a transfer that was only possible through state direction and control. It showed us that class power matters when it comes to money and finance. It is real, it is ruthless, and it is protected by the state.

The purpose of this book is to expand upon and interrogate these issues. In doing so, it will make the following points:

- Money is a social technology, one that underpins a complex system of social relations, and the ownership and control of that technology gives those who hold it enormous social, economic and political power.

- There is a class in Ireland that has carved out a niche for itself within that system at a national and international level, and that class is deeply embedded in the institutions of the state.

- There are alternatives, but they involve facing up to both the deep economic class divisions within Irish society and the gendered nature of economic inequality, as well as working collectively to transform the institutions and ideas which sustain and reproduce those divisions.

The first chapter will look at how money, defined as a social technology, underpins a complex system of human relationships. Money cannot be separated from the society in which it operates. It is not a thing in itself but a mechanism for dealing with issues of social organisation and distribution, and one that is subject to conflicting interests. It gives support to, and is supported by, a dense network of institutions, systems and cultural practices that are themselves beholden to deeply unequal relationships of gender, power and authority.

These inequalities do not happen by accident. They are not some afterthought, but rather the result of how we constitute our social, economic and political worlds. The ownership of that technology and the control of the system gives those who hold it enormous power. Since the seventeenth century this technology has increasingly fallen under the influence of capitalism.

Capitalism did not invent money. It adapted it for its own purposes, in particular its obsession with the search for yield, that is, the search for a profitable return on investment, with that return expressed in money form. The investment can be returned as an interest payment, a dividend or a claim on profit. Money put to such use is known as 'capital'. When capitalism invests in chickens it does not want more chickens; it wants more money, which it then reinvests in order to make more money. The purpose of capitalism, therefore, is self-expansion: capital begets capital. In the words of Immanuel Wallerstein, it is this 'relentless and curiously self-regarding goal of the holder of capital, the accumulation of still more capital, and the relations this holder of capital had therefore to establish with other persons in order to achieve this goal, which we denominate as capitalist'.[14]

Capital (money as investment) is not the only use of money, but it is the use that today dominates our money and financial systems. As such, any discussion about money must include a discussion on capital and the social and political system of capitalism that prioritises its own self-expansion.

This leads us to the second chapter, which has as its focus the issue of money and capital and the Irish state. It places Ireland within the international financial system and outlines the role that the Irish state has carved out for itself within that system. Money under capitalism is a distinctly class-based relationship, and in order to understand how money works in Ireland, and in whose interests, we need to have an understanding of economic class power and relationships in the state. It will make the argument that Ireland is dominated by the interests of an indigenous comprador, or middleman class. This is not a new class within Irish society, nor is it a new relationship. It is one that routes itself through the very structure of the state and has done so since its formation in 1922. This class acts as an intermediary between the resources of the state and the interests of foreign capital. In the past the middlemen were strongest in the cattle industry, finance, construction and real estate. Today their presence is most keenly felt in stockbroking, accountancy, law and property speculation. Today it is our tax code that is openly traded, and for those involved it is a highly profitable business.

The focus on money and the state is based on a particular reading of the role and purpose of the state under capitalism. 'Absolute private property, the contractual relation that binds producer to appropriator, the process of commodity exchange,' wrote the historian Ellen Meiksins Wood, 'all these require the legal forms, the coercive apparatus, the policing functions of the state.'[15] Capitalism needs the state in order to function and survive. It needs the state to protect it from its own internal contradictions. It is not surprising, then, that capitalism actively shapes the state to serve its own interests. This is a crucial point as we move into ways to combat economic class power in Ireland. To return to William K. Tabb, an economic crisis allows us to see the true nature of financial and political power, and we should use it as such.

The third chapter looks at a framework of ideas that might inform a unifying strategy for progressive change in Ireland. The central thesis of the book is that money is a social activity underpinned by economic class relations and alternatives to the present money system in Ireland will have to confront class power in order to have any chance of success. This is not an easy thing to do. It requires organisation in the workplace, the community and the political sphere, as well as tackling the gendered and racial inequalities produced by capitalism. This chapter will explore these issues in more detail, but is focused on progressive forces in Ireland organising collectively in order to combat deeply embedded Irish moneyed interests. It presents a framework for thinking about alternatives and organisation rather than the alternatives themselves.

This book sets out to provide a scholarly (and hopefully readable) analysis of money and capital, the institutional economic class interests that exist in Ireland and alternatives in the spheres of paid labour and social reproduction. It is a political work in that it picks a side in the debate and hopefully shows why I have reached my conclusions. I hope to educate and inform and I also hope to persuade. In that sense this book is a polemic; it has something to say about our world and it does not apologise for saying it.

It is hoped that the analysis laid out here will be treated as a starting point for the reader's own individual exploration of the topic of money and finance. I have certain views on the subject and I will lay them down, but they are by no means the last word and should not be taken as such. The overall purpose is to bring money and the money system into the debate around alternatives. The book's singular focus on that topic should not be taken as an argument for a singular causality: that the money system is somehow the cause of all our woes and that a change in that system will change everything. I do not believe that. Capitalism did not invent the money system. That system was appropriated by capitalism and shaped to serve its own particular interests.

The Canadian economist Jim Stanford wrote that 'a society in which ordinary people know more about economics, and recognize the often conflicting interests at stake in the economy, is a society in which more people will feel confident deciding for themselves what's best – instead of trusting the experts'.[16] In his view greater knowledge of economics makes for a more democratic society, and I believe this to be true. At the same time, education alone will not solve the problem. An awareness of the issues and an understanding of their importance is an essential part of any transformative goal, but it is not enough on its own to actually change the situation. Education that is divorced from organisation and direction is akin to Oscar Wilde's remarkable rocket that explodes in a fanfare appreciated by nobody but itself.

Ideas are important, but they only come alive through action. Every idea of social change needs a strategy.

The political space is a contested space between capital accumulation and democratic ideals. One side is winning at the moment, but it is certainly possible it will swing back the other way in the future. For that to happen, though, people have to take a side. At the same time, as the educator and social activist Myles Horton once said, 'You need to know *why* you take sides; you should be able to justify it.'[17] This brings us to the Síreacht series of books, which aims to provoke thought and discussion on matters of received wisdom and common sense, as well as providing practical alternatives to the way we operate and organise. It is one that is committed to the exposition of alternative perspectives on society and critiques of received wisdom. This book is a modest contribution to that process.

Money

INTRODUCTION

There are three parts to this chapter. It will look at the nature of money, the emergence of capitalism in the seventeenth century and the way that it adopted the money system for its own purposes, and it will then jump forward three hundred years to the modern world and explore the dynamic between money and capitalism today. The purpose of this is to debunk some myths and to shine a light on the true nature of money; to make clear the relationship between capitalism and the money system; and to show how that relationship currently operates, with particular emphasis on the role of the state in protecting capitalism's objectives and interests. In doing so, it is preparing the ground for Chapter 2, which is an exploration of money and the Irish state. Taken together, they provide the context for the final chapter, which will explore organisational strategies for a more equitable and progressive Ireland.

WHAT IS MONEY?

Money is a human invention. It is not a gift from the gods or a by-product of nature, nor is it found in a hole in the ground. It is a social technology, one of the oldest we have. In the words of the academic Geoffrey Ingham, it was the basis, along with numeracy and writing, 'for the world's first large-scale complex societies in the ancient Near East during the third millennium BC'.[18] It owes its existence to people and to the dynamics of social organisation, exchange and circulation. Without these elements, money is nothing.

Money allows for the movement of obligations, possessions, goods, services, promises, debts and legacies between people. It is 'a mode of mobilizing resources', wrote the historian Christine Desan, 'one that communities design for that end and individuals appropriate for their own purposes'.[19] For this to happen, things of value must be expressed in monetary terms and have the ability to be converted into money. This process is not always equal, not always democratic, and if unchecked, social wealth once monetised will congeal around a very small but powerful section of society. The money system contains within it the ability to concentrate social value in the hands of a few, even though such value is created through the actions of many. When we start to look at the money system *as a system*, it becomes clear that 'there is more to the history of money than just buying and selling'.[20]

Money cannot be comprehended in isolation, as a

thing in itself. To see the form that money takes – be it notes, coins or bank account digits – and not the societal dynamics that underpin that form, is to miss entirely the purpose, structure and power of money and the money system. It is dependent on law, as well as public and private institutions such as central banks, government departments, commercial banks and financial markets. It cannot transcend its social and legal setting and remain as money. The modern Irish pound was in effect from 1927 to 2002. Its main value today is to collectors on eBay.

Money is not neutral. It has powerful distributional effects. It operates simultaneously through the realms of value, law and time. It is abstract and powerful, and actively shapes the world it inhabits. We can lend it, work for it, win it, steal it, borrow it or receive it through various supports, but in order to maintain ourselves we need to get our hands on it. This involuntary compulsion to attain money, the coercive power that the money nexus wields, is in sharp contrast to the view that the desire for money is one of greed and little else. We need money to survive, and for most people that is compulsion enough.

Money is social and political. It only comes alive through a dynamic between people, institutions, law and the state. We see it as a thing (notes and coins) but we experience it as an activity (buying, selling, working, renting, saving, lending, investing, etc.). A man on a desert island who sits on a pile of gold coins is waiting for a ship to arrive, so he can put them to use. The coins on the island will not make corn cultivate itself, or through their mere presence turn metal into a spear. Money viewed as separate from society is the same as words separate from grammar; it is babble, etchings without meaning. We cannot focus solely on the mere 'words' of money (notes, coins, digits) if we want to understand it; we also need to study its 'grammar', that is, the underlying structure that gives money its expressive and interpretative logic.

Societies change, and the structural dynamic and focus of money changes with them. The world we live in today is a capitalist world. We may still use essentially the same type of money forms as ancient and feudal societies – coins, credit notes, paper currency – but that does not mean we use them in the same way, or for entirely the same purposes. The logic of money does not come from money itself; it is a societal logic and that changes over time.

Capitalism has its own logic, of course, the essence of which is the hunt for yield (return on investment). That is its core organisational principle. It monetises human activity and natural resources based on the presumption that such monetisation will produce a profitable return. It transforms societies and devours people and nature to meet this objective. As a result, in terms of our discussion here, we need to talk about both money *and* capitalism. They are inseparable in the world we live in today, but first we need to dispel some myths.

> *[If a man borrows silver] he shall weigh and deliver his silver and the interest on it at the harvest.*
> Laws of Hammurabi, *c.* 1750 BCE, Babylon[21]

The emergence of money is often explained by the limits of barter as a form of exchange. A cobbler wants a chicken, but the farmer does not want shoes. They cannot swap their goods, so the cobbler has a bright idea and gives the farmer a token. With this token the farmer can go off and get the things he needs. 'The first difficulty in barter is to find two persons whose disposable possessions mutually suit each other's wants,' said the economist William Stanley Jevons.[22] 'There may be many people wanting, and many possessing those things wanted,' he wrote, 'but to allow of an act of barter, there must be a double coincidence, which will rarely happen.'[23] Barter is an on-the-spot transaction. I have what you want, and you have what I want (a 'double coincidence' of wants), so we both agree to swap.

The absence of such a double coincidence, the story goes, leads to the use of a third commodity that people will accept in order to part with their goods. They do so in the knowledge that the third commodity can be used for the purchase of goods at a later date. This third commodity – in this case a token – is being used as a medium of exchange. It plays an intermediary role in the transfer of goods and services. It allows buyers and sellers to 'fit' each other in ways simply not possible under barter. The use of a medium of exchange is a central part of all modern societies. We know it today as money.

There are many problems with this explanation for the origin of money. First of all, how does a cobbler get to be a cobbler solely through barter? How come it is only after his apprenticeship and years of decent living that he is finally confronted with a non-barter quandary when he is in search of a chicken but only finds a well-shod farmer? The logic breaks down under even the most cursory examination, yet the fundamental problem is not just its lack of logic but the fact that it is simply not true. It never happened. Money did not come out of a breakdown in a double coincidence of wants. 'No example of a barter economy, pure and simple, has ever been described, let alone the emergence from it of money,' wrote the historical anthropologist Caroline Humphrey. In fact 'all available ethnography suggests that there never has been such a thing'.[24] There are historical instances of barter, usually between strangers, but no ancient society had barter as its primary form of exchange, that is, barter as the fundamental organisational principle around which intra-societal exchange took place. None.[25]

The dilemma raised by the story of the non-existent farmer and the cobbler – I have something you want *at this moment*, but you do not have something I want *at this moment* – was solved by ancient societies through a simple mechanism: credit. The separation of the act of final payment from the act of exchange allowed the exchange to take place immediately. There was no need for a scramble for equivalents, only an acknowledgement that the payment was now a debt, and that debt would be settled at a later date. The two-dimensional world of instant give and receive was transformed by the addition of a third dimension: time.

We have no idea when this innovation first arose as it predates writing. We know it is earlier than literacy because the earliest writings we have relate to the recording of credit and debt relations. The elongation of the settlement of payment via an obligation to pay mechanism gave complex human societies the space to expand and function. Even today, the breakdown of this mechanism will cause a society to crash. The tools may change but the innovation, paradoxically, stays the same.

Over 4,000 years ago debt contracts were drawn up in Mesopotamia that were interest-bearing obligations, 'the issuing of which was rewarding to the creditor, and the receipt of which may have been an economic necessity for the debtor'.[26] The laws of Hammurabi from *c.* 1750 BCE recorded some of the terms and conditions. For example, 'if a merchant gives grain or silver as an interest-bearing loan, he shall take 100 silas of grain per kur as interest; if he gives silver as an interest-bearing loan, he shall take 36 barleycorns per shekel of silver as interest'.[27] Interest-free loans, usually of less than one month, were also used and appear to have been common among extended families and groups of professionals.[28] A third class of loans were paid back not with silver or barley, but with human labour, usually at harvest time. These were also interest-bearing. The labour delivered was in excess of the value of the principal.

The issuing of loans was not limited to one class of people: 'A debtor might owe an obligation to the temple of one of the chief gods of the pantheon, to a member of the royal family, to an urban entrepreneur, or to a relative or co-worker.'[29] The power to lend was open to any household with the means to do so: 'The individual

creditor ... was usually the head of an urban household with access to surplus wealth, usually in silver or barley, which could be loaned out in both short and long term agreements.'[30]

All of this was done without coin or currency as we know it. Nor were the Mesopotamians swapping chickens for shoes. They had a detailed and effective credit system that operated without recourse to a physical currency. They operated a fully functioning monetary system that worked because they had a standard for the measurement of value against which debts and obligations were calculated. They had what is called today a 'unit of account' – a yardstick for measuring value – the job of which in modern society is carried out by a currency such as the euro, dollar or yen. One euro is one unit of the accounting system we use to compare and measure the value of things against each other. The Mesopotamians may have used more than one item as their unit of account – barley and silver, for example, in the city of Ur – but the complexity of the value-measurement system was not an issue as the economic, cultural and social nuances were understood by those who used it.

The monetary function of barley and silver contains elements we recognise today. They were adapted as 'units of account', that is, as standards for the measurement of value for the purposes of settling debts and obligations. They were also utilised as a means of payment – that is settling accounts, not merely measuring them – and they allowed individual households and the city hierarchy to engage in economic, social and cultural activities of distribution, redistribution and financial advancement, across space and time. We should not assume that the Mesopotamians somehow invented the concept of the unit of account as 'a way of comparing things mathematically, as proportion: of saying one of X is equivalent to six of Y'.[31] It is just that the earliest examples we have today come from excavations of the ancient city of Ur, but the concept itself 'is probably as old as human thought'.[32]

The settlement of debts was not confined to market transactions. Money in so-called primitive societies was not used simply to facilitate market transactions. It was also used 'to arrange marriages, establish the paternity of children, head off feuds, console mourners at funerals, seek forgiveness in the case of crimes, negotiate treaties, acquire followers'.[33] Here, money was being used 'as a social currency, to create, maintain, or sever relations between people rather than to purchase things'.[34] For example, in the case of early Christian Ireland there were two units of account – the *sét* and the *cumal* – which were used to quantify the value of social obligations as well as fines for 'injury, murder, improper distraint, improper use of legal procedure, trespass, theft, cutting down protected trees, and so forth'.[35] The *sét* and the *cumal* simply measured the debt; cattle, silver and grain were used as actual payment.

Three thousand years separate the Mesopotamian city of Ur and early Christian Ireland, but each had its own way of measuring value and settling debts of a social and financial nature. The object that was used to measure values (unit of account) was not necessarily the object used to settle the debt (means of payment). Again, the complexity was not an issue as long as people understood the measurements and accepted the payments. It shows, however, that credit, debt and the measurement of each, as mental concepts and societal relations, predate coin and what we consider today as money. Furthermore, payments relating to social obligations were just as important as market-based ones.

The highlighted examples – and there are many others[36] – show that units of account (measurement) and means of payment (settlement) were developed as practical solutions to societal dynamics. They arose out of the everyday actions and interactions of people. They did not arise out of barter and they were not contingent on coin. Neither did they exist only when there was a market need for them. It was not just the exchange of goods but the settlement of societal debts and obligations that gave rise to an agreed accounting system to facilitate that process.

Money, therefore, is a *societal* need. It is also used for market exchange for sure, but it is in essence a technology that allows people to smooth their relationships with each other in complex societal structures, be they ancient settlements of Mesopotamia, rural settlements of early Christian Ireland, or present-day globalised cities such as Tokyo, London or New York. The unit of account and means of payment are codified through specific laws and accountancy structures that vary from society to society, but the concepts and their application are universal and human.

The earliest examples we have of a codified debt and credit system with a unit of account as a standard measure of value is from 4,000 years ago, and that is purely down to the survival of written records. It is highly unlikely that these systems arrived at precisely the same time they were written down. With the concepts of credit, debt and units of account we are in all likelihood dealing with something that is as fundamental to human existence as language. The advent of coin around 700 BCE brought a new element to the dynamic, not because of the metal that was used but because of the authority that was, literally, stamped on it. Whereas the history of credit is social, the history of coin is, in essence, the history of state power.

And they brought it, and He said unto them, 'Whose image and superscription is this?' And they said unto Him, 'Caesar's'.

Mark 12:16

The political project of the physical currency of coin was to centralise all the key aspects of the monetary system – unit of account, means of payment, store of value and medium of exchange – into one exclusive physical expression under the control of a state power. The advantage to those in power was clear. For example, Rome paid its soldiers in coin. It also demanded taxes from its regions to be paid in that coin. The regions, in order to get the coins to pay their taxes, had to accept Roman coin from soldiers as payment for goods. Rome may have been getting back the same pieces of stamped metal it sent out, but in the process, it was getting its armies fed and supplied by the local population, all for the cost of manufacture and distribution of coin.

But this is not an easy project to pursue as the techniques of measuring value through an accepted standard, and settling debts against that benchmark, are not imbued in the coin but are instead an integral output of human societal relations and will spring up whenever and wherever needed. Neither is it inevitable that the item used to measure value will be the item used to make payments and settle debts. It took hundreds of years to finally bed down coin as the consolidated expression of the monetary system, that is, the one item that could be used for all four actions: measurement, settlement, storage and exchange. It also took a lot of killing. Coin as money – as the one, true, embodiment of the monetary system as a whole – was a bloody, coercive act of political and state agency.

The slow collapse of the Roman Empire saw coin incorporated into the emerging power blocs in Europe. 'The barbarian allies [of Rome], although they had no tradition of coinage of their own,' wrote the historian Peter Spufford, 'took over the Roman mints in the western provinces of the empire, and continued to strike coins at them in the names of the emperors.'[37] The barbarian kings kept the Roman taxation system at first, adjusting it to their own purposes, but in the absence of a functioning state administration it slowly fell into decay.[38] This had consequences for the use of coin, as the payment of taxes was the primary force driving its circulation. By the end of the sixth century, Pope Gregory I was taking rents in grain that had previously been paid in coin. In Britain the withdrawal of Roman forces and the expulsion of Roman officials hastened the breakdown in administrative contacts with the rest of the empire and by 435 CE, 'coin ceased to be used there as a medium of exchange. Not for 200 years, until the seventh century, were coins again used in Britain as money, although many survived as jewellery, or were used for gifts or for compensation.'[39] The moneyness of a coin (this is, the ability of a coin to be treated as money) is not intrinsic to the coin. Moneyness is an attribute conferred by society, in practical terms by a state or a state-like authority. Once society moves on, moneyness goes with it.

The demise of coin in Britain, and its moribund status in mainland Europe, did not mean an end to economic and social activity across the continent. It did pose significant challenges, however, for the various power blocs that stepped into the vacuum caused by the decline of empire. In order to give coin the authority it lacked as a result of a barely functioning state apparatus, a greater emphasis was placed on the materiality of the coin rather than the face of the king it carried. Christine Desan wrote that the 'medieval world struggled for centuries to make money out of commodities [such as gold, silver and copper]. Selecting a commodity material, competing for its supply, minting it into coin, maintaining that coin in circulation, structuring denominations, securing small change for everyday use, protecting money from fraud

– all were immense challenges.'[40] It is during this period that the idea that the moneyness of a coin is contained in its metal – the assumption that 'money is simply the commodity [the metal] it contains'[41] – really begins to take shape in Europe. The significance of this shift in thinking is that money became associated more with the thing that was used as money (coin), rather than with the governing authority that it *represented*.

Coins need to circulate in order to work as a medium of exchange, but if a coin is believed to have a value (due to its metal content) that is equal to or greater than its representative value (which is stamped on it and enforced by a higher state authority), hoarding will take place and circulation will decrease.[42] The hoarding was not just of the moneyness of the coin (for example, money as savings) but also of the metal used to make it. 'As a result,' wrote Fernand Braudel, 'the engine was constantly being deprived of fuel.'[43] The fashion of metal as money gave rise somewhat to alchemy, the dream of turning base metal into gold – to transform a metal of lower value into something of higher value, to 'make money' where it did not exist before. It eluded these proto-chemists for centuries. Meanwhile the Chinese arrived at their own way of 'making money'. They swapped metal for paper and gave it the ruler's authority. In other words, they printed it.

It appears that the first Chinese notes were issued around 650 CE, but the practice did not become widespread until the Song dynasty of 960–1279 CE.[44] These were not currency notes as we would know them but 'privately issued remittance, credit or exchange notes with a date limitation. The first paper money as we know and use it today (that is, officially issued exchange notes, with no date limitation) were the exchange certificates of the Jin in 1189.'[45] Paper currency was the only authorised currency during the Mongol Yuan dynasty (1206–1367 CE). The Venetian merchant Marco Polo visited China towards the latter end of the thirteenth century and wrote a brief overview of the monetary system of Kublai Khan:

All these cards are stamped with his seal ... He makes all his payments in them, and circulates them through the kingdoms and provinces over which he holds dominion; and none dares to refuse them under pain of death ... The merchants often bring to him goods worth 400,000 bezants, and he pays them all in these cards, which they willingly accept, because they can make purchases with them throughout the whole empire ... When any of the cards are torn or spoiled, the owner carries them to the place whence they were issued, and receives fresh ones, with a deduction of 3 per cent. If a man wishes gold or silver to make plate, girdles, or other ornaments, he goes to the office, carrying a sufficient number of cards, and gives them in payment for the quantity which he requires.'[46]

Marco Polo also noted that 'all the Khan's armies are paid with this sort of money'.[47] The paper currency had authority because of the power of the emperor and the state apparatus that administered and enforced his rule. Khan used currency to fund his armies in much the same way as Rome; it was only the form, not the content, that was different. There was no political state in Europe at this time, with its fragmented lines and petty aristocracies, that was in a position to command the seal of authority that was necessary to make a paper currency work. This does not mean that there was an absence of paper notes. It was the private banks, however, not the royal courts, that embraced the technology.

Banking as we recognise it first emerged as a specialised profession in the northern Italian city-states of the thirteenth century. They took up paper methods such as bills of exchange and written instructions as means of payment and adapted them for their own purposes. They also financed the multiple wars of the period, often both sides at the same time. 'Without Italian bankers Charles of Anjou could not have conquered Sicily nor Edward I Wales, papal wars would have ground to a halt, and the kings of France and England would have wanted means to begin the struggle culminating in the Hundred Years War.'[48] The banking dynasties of the Frescobaldi, the Franzesi, and the Gallerani were installed in high positions in the courts of England, France and Flanders. The warring factions of medieval Europe found themselves in common alliance with Italian finance.

It is with the credit mechanisms and profit-seeking strategies of the Italian banks that we can start to identify a nascent form of capitalist activity (such as private-bank credit being used as investment where the return on investment is delivered in money form). Unlike in China, the use of credit-paper within European commercial networks was outside the state apparatus, yet it was still linked to it through the use of the same unit of account (currency) for the measurement of value. The Italian banks did not issue a new currency; they issued a new form of credit note that was linked to the currency and in its own specific way almost as powerful in terms of its ability to settle debts.

At first the bills of exchange and IOUs issued by the banks were linked to a particular debtor. They soon became accepted, however, in terms of their face value. Once this happened, the initial debt behind the note became 'anonymous'; that is, it could be used by the holder as currency because it would be accepted in certain circumstances as payment. It was no longer the obligation of one particular person to settle the debt but the bank itself. The funds for the payment came from the bank's own accounts, not from the funds of the person named on the IOU. 'Signifiers of debt became transferable to third parties and could circulate as private money within commercial networks.'[49] 'For the very first time,' wrote the sociologist Geoffrey Ingham,

the *extensive* production of a form of money took place outside the state's monopoly of currency issue. Eventually, such signifiers of debt became completely *depersonalised* (that is, payable to "X" or "bearer") and were issued as *bank money*; that is to say, the promises to pay drawn on banks became a widely accepted means of payment. With this change, the *private* capitalistic financing of enterprise on a large scale became a possibility.'[50]

According to Ingham the essence of capitalism lies here, in 'the elastic creation of money by means of readily transferable debt'.[51] It would be another four hundred years, however, before it would develop into a fully operational social, economic and political system but the key concept had been tried and tested. Banks could create credit-money of their own, independent of the deposits they held, have it accepted by commercial and state entities, and deliver a profitable return that was expressed in money form.

The ability to have its own private credit notes accepted as currency gave banking enormous potential to influence the shape and direction of European states. However, bank credit-money was only as secure as the issuing bank and the private credit networks. As Ingham said, 'they were only as strong as the networks of commerce in which they were embedded. Defaults on repayments broke the chains in the banking system's expansion of credit by causing bankruptcies and triggering recessions.'[52] The next major turning point came when local and state administrations and merchants stepped in to guarantee the private credit-money through the formation of a public debt based on its issuance. This is the innovation that moved bank credit notes from a financial technology into a financial and political system.

The first experiment in this process occurred in

Venice in 1487 when the city introduced a public bank. It was then taken up in the Netherlands in 1609 with the formation of the Bank of Amsterdam, which 'helped to make Amsterdam the principal money market in Europe for nearly two centuries'.[53] It is the creation of the Bank of England in 1694, however, that saw the use of private credit as capital brought to a truly national and international stage.

CAPITALISM AND THE MONEY SYSTEM

I am not a great lord nor a capitalist; I am poor and happy.

Jean-Jacques Rousseau, 1759 [54]

I have referenced capitalism more than once at this stage, but what exactly is it? Money, trade, markets – all of these go back thousands of years and arose in some form or another in almost every society across the planet. Yet capitalism itself, in global historical terms, is a relatively new phenomenon with quite specific geographical and historical origins, limited to a small number of European states in the sixteenth and seventeenth centuries. 'No reasonable person would deny that in Asia, Africa, and the Americas, there were high civilisations, which in some cases developed commercial practices, as well as technological advances of various kinds that far surpassed those of medieval England,' wrote Ellen Meiksins Wood, 'but the emergence of capitalism is difficult to explain precisely because it bears no relation to prior superiority or more advanced development in commercial sophistication, science and technology, or ... material wealth.'[55] In other words, there is nothing in the history of Europe to suggest that capitalism was inevitable, that it was a natural progression from the modes of social organisation and production that preceded it. Whatever led to capitalism was specific to the political, cultural, economic and social dynamics that pertained to the Netherlands and England in the early modern era. The only way that capitalism could be construed as 'natural' and 'inevitable' is for the history of those two countries to be somehow the 'natural' and 'inevitable' progression of all humanity – something with which those colonised by them might have a slight issue.

Overall, Wood defines capitalism as 'a system in which all major economic actors are dependent on the market for their basic requirements of life ... [where] wage labourers have to sell their labour power to a capitalist simply in order to gain access to the means of their own life and even the means of their own labour; and the capitalist depends on the market for access to labour and to realize the profits the workers produce'.[56] Under capitalism, human relations are mediated through markets, a process that capitalism depends upon, and one that is itself a process of *monetisation*. People sell their labour power in order to attain money, so they can then access human necessities that have themselves been monetised and marketised. The money nexus is what binds it all together.

Why is this the case? Why is capitalism obsessed with the monetisation of human labour and social relations, as well as nature itself? The issue relates to that which is specific to capitalism, that which makes it different from the other forms of social organisation that came before it. 'The production of goods and services is subordinate to the production of capital and capitalist profit,' says Wood, because the 'basic objective of the capitalist system ... is the production and self-expansion of capital'.[57] The purpose of capital within capitalism is to make more of itself. The products and services produced are *not* the end goal; they are simply the means to an end.

The same point was made by Immanuel Wallerstein. 'Historical capitalism', he wrote in 1983, is 'that concrete, time-bounded, space-bounded integrated locus of productive activities within which the endless accumulation of capital has been the economic objective or "law" that has governed or prevailed in fundamental economic activity'.[58] The end-goal of capitalism – to accumulate more capital – was, in Wallerstein's eyes, a patently absurd one. 'Capitalists are like white mice on a treadmill, running ever faster in order to run still faster,' he wrote, 'in the process, no doubt, some people live well, but others live miserably; and how well, and for how long, do those who live well live?'[59] The genesis of this bizarre and psychotic historical system was late-fifteenth-century Europe. Over the next four hundred years it expanded under the guise of free trade, with colonialism as its battering ram, and 'today covers the entire globe'.[60] As to the bizarreness of capitalism, it was a contemporary of witch trials, after all, and each shared a logic with the other.[61]

That the early modern European era was the birthplace of capitalism is echoed by the economist Joseph A. Schumpeter in his 1954 posthumous publication, *History of Economic Analysis*. He wrote that, owing to the importance of finance to capitalist production and trade, the development by banks of 'negotiable paper and of created deposits afford perhaps the best indication we have for dating the rise of capitalism. Around the Mediterranean both emerged in the course of the fourteenth century, though negotiability was not fully established before the sixteenth.'[62] 'Notwithstanding the importance of the free market, machine technology, factory organisation and labour-capital relations,' wrote Geoffrey Ingham, 'the historical specificity of capitalism is also to be found in its distinctive credit-money system.'[63] The way that banks and the private-credit system developed in Europe, *at the time that they did*, was key to the overall development of capitalism as a social, economic and political system.

The essence of a bank consists in credit.

Henry Maxwell, 1721[64]

At the time of capital's first emergence in thirteenth-century Italy the dominant view in Europe of what constituted wealth was land. It was the soil, and control over the ownership and produce of the soil, that made for kings and princes and knights of the court. Three hundred years later the idea was still to the fore. 'The principal advantage and foundation of trade in England is raised from the wealth which is gained out of the produce of the earth,' wrote Sir Josiah Child, head of the East India Company.[65] Wealth was seen as natural and found in nature; international trade was therefore a form of war for the procurement of finite riches.[66]

Into this world came the idea that the source of all wealth in human society was not land or gold or silver but human labour, the work of human hands transforms into money through market exchange. 'We may increase our people by multitudes, and grow infinitely rich by them too,' wrote the English politician Carew Reynell in 1674, 'for it is a sad case that there should be so many lusty poor about everywhere, and yet so many manufactures want to be brought in, which would set at work millions of people more than we have to spare.'[67]

Reynell, along with his contemporaries in England, looked to the Netherlands and sought to emulate it. He believed that manufacturing and banking should be allowed to develop and expand in England – as they had in Amsterdam – as this would 'not only increase people but also trade, and advance it', adding, 'I wish some great persons would make it their business to look after such great things.'[68] The sentiments were echoed by the Scottish economist John Law, who argued for the replacement of metallic money with paper money. 'Domestic trade depends on money,' he wrote, 'a greater quantity employs more people than a lesser quantity.'[69] The credit creation afforded through paper currency would provide new finance to increase economic activity in production and trade.

One of the key dynamics in the emergence of capitalism was the rise of a banking and merchant class whose economic base and profit-seeking strategies were different to, and in conflict with, those of landholders. The political structure at the time, not only in England but across Europe, was predicated on the ownership of landed property. The legal structure followed suit. The state was geared towards the interests of land and princes. The rise of capitalism as an economic force chipped away at the political and economic status quo, first in Amsterdam, then in London. One of the ways it was able to do this was through the ability of private banks to create credit notes and have them treated as state money, what we see today as currency.

Bank credit, in order to truly function, needs a coercive element. Society provides one through the courts and the law. This is usually expressed through a claim on the assets of the debtor – the assets valorising the credit in lieu of the failure of valorisation through the action 'funded' by the credit. But in order for that to work, the coercive element needs to be able to sanction the debtor to sufficient degree. This was extremely difficult for banks to do when the debtor was a prince or a king. The establishment of the Bank of England in 1694 helped to change that through 'a compromise that expressed the delicate balance between too much and too little royal power'.[70]

The overthrow of James II in the Glorious Revolution of 1688 brought with it a reordering of political economy. King James II was an advocate of the political philosophy of Sir Josiah Child and the Tory faction of British politics, which saw land as the ultimate source of wealth and a finite resource. The new king, William of Orange, was backed by the Whig faction which was comprised mainly of traders, manufacturers and financiers. The dominant thinking among this group was that 'property was created by human endeavour and that banks could do much to increase the nation's wealth'.[71] The limits of wealth were simply the limits of human energy and ambition. Furthermore, the revolution saw England engaged in the war of the Grand Alliance against France. King William had to fund his troops, and the preferred solution of the Whigs was via public debt issued by a national bank.

Traditionally, kings were immune from legal prosecution for any non-payment of their personal debts. In 1672, for example, King Charles II defaulted on monies owed to London's mercantile class. Through a confluence of circumstances that same class was in a position in 1689 to install a king, only this time it ensured that all additional royal revenues had to be approved by parliament. In 1694, with King William once again in desperate need of funds, they established the Bank of England with an initial outlay of £1.2m in bank stock. This was used to create a credit loan at 8 per cent interest, which was made out to the state, and not to the king personally. In other words, the credit loan was structured in such a way that it was valorised through a tax stream that was guaranteed by the state and not personally by the king. The sovereign's personal debt was made a public debt. The state was now 'financed by loans from a powerful creditor class that were channelled through a public bank'.[72] The bank, for its part, got government debt paper that could be used as an additional asset for the creation of credit that was, in all important respects, backed by a state guarantee.

Private credit production and public currency production were now merged. 'For the first time, bank currency written against public debt circulated.'[73] The Bank of England loan created a long-term funded public debt and facilitated a widely circulating credit-currency. As Ingham notes, 'the institutions for the production of capitalist credit-money, and the balance of economic and political interests that underpinned it, were beginning to take shape'.[74]

Capitalism monetises labour power, social value and nature in order to secure a return on investment. In contrast to the wealth produced by the monetisation of land through rent, the wealth that is produced by the monetisation of human labour is open-ended. It is not subject to the same investment limitations as land. Capital investment in monetised human output is an extremely fluid dynamic. The process is supported by a specific social, political, legal, financial and industrial system, elements of which arose in the Italian city-states of the thirteenth century and were further developed in Amsterdam in the 1600s but came to fruition in England towards the end of the seventeenth century.

In order to grow, capitalism needs a wage-labour force, that is, a constant and growing supply of workers who have nothing to sell but their labour power. Such a labour force was not the norm in seventeenth-century England; it had to be created. 'These newly freed men became sellers of themselves only after they had been robbed of all of their own means of production,' wrote Marx, 'and this history, the history of their expropriation, is written in the annals of mankind in letters of blood and fire.'[75] The creation of a new class of wage-labour brought with it a class conflict between those who sell their labour and those who purchase it. This conflict was at the very beginning of capitalism as a social system, and it is still there today. It is inherent to capitalism. Sometimes it can be mediated, but it cannot be eliminated.

Capitalism's creation of a wage-labour workforce was also highly gendered. 'The exploitation of women has played a central function in the process of capitalist accumulation,' wrote Silvia Federici, 'insofar as women have been the producers and reproducers of the most essential capitalist commodity: labour power.'[76] The unpaid labour of women in the home 'has been the pillar upon which the exploitation of the waged workers, "waged slavery", has been built, and the secret of its productivity'.[77] We will return to this in the final chapter, when we look at alternatives and organisational strategies, but for now it is enough to see that 'capitalism exploits more work and production relations than just wage labour relations'.[78] Capitalism is not just an economic framework, it is a political and social project that involves the fundamental reorganisation of societies and peoples in order to achieve its prime objective: capital accumulation. This brings with it class conflict and gendered inequalities.

The final part of this chapter will look at capitalism from the Second World War to the present day. The reason for this timeframe is that after the war a 'social contract' was effectively signed between capital and labour in the US and certain European countries, which saw social democracy mediate the class antagonism within capitalism. By the mid-1970s this had started to break down, sowing the seeds for the 2008 crisis and the onslaught of austerity.

Throughout this period, the financial system played a critical role in protecting capital accumulation as much as it could from the redistributive policies of social democracy (particularly through tax avoidance and the establishment of off-shore centres). And as we will see in Chapter 3, Ireland had a not insignificant part to play in this world of tax havens and loose regulation, to the detriment of its own citizens and, indeed, to the state itself.

MONEY AND CAPITALISM TODAY

... to drive only the usurious money lenders from the temple of international finance ...

Henry Morgenthau, Jr, 1944[79]

On 1 July 1944 the United Nations Monetary and Financial Conference began its proceedings at the Mount Washington Hotel, Bretton Woods, New Hampshire. It was the most important international gathering of its kind since the Paris Peace Conference of 1919, with 730 delegates from forty-four countries.[80] It was less than a month since the Allied invasion of Normandy and seventeen months since the obliteration of Germany's sixth army at Stalingrad. The impetus behind the meeting, however, was not so much the impending collapse of Nazi Germany but the desire to find a way to curb the social and political destruction wrought by the unrestrained movement of capital.

The previous thirty years had seen two world wars, a great depression, revolution in Russia and the collapse of both the Ottoman and Austro-Hungarian empires. Economic nationalism and currency policies of the 1930s had set the scene for the outbreak of war in 1939. The Bretton Wood delegates were set with the task of devising 'a durable institutional architecture for global monetary affairs, an architecture capable of facilitating a massive increase in international trade'.[81] Three months earlier a technical group of experts from Canada, China, France, Great Britain and the United States had issued a joint statement on the desirability of an international monetary fund to regulate the supply, demand and trade of capital between nations.[82] The conference was called to devise practical ways of creating such a mechanism. The documents signed at the end of the proceedings became known collectively as the Bretton Woods Agreement.

The new system created an international currency exchange rate mechanism predicated on the dollar and allowed the use of capital controls by individual states. It also established the International Monetary Fund (IMF) and the International Bank for Reconstruction and Development (later the World Bank). Although it quickly came to be dominated by US and Wall Street interests, the Bretton Woods system was a rejection of the type of liberal financial policies that had destabilised the world since 1929. It was a radical departure that 'had its roots in a kind of socio-ideological structural break that took place across the industrial world in the wake of the economic and financial crises of the early 1930s', wrote the historian Eric Helleiner.[83] The 'private and central bankers who had dominated financial politics in the 1920s' were 'largely discredited by the crisis' and were 'increasingly replaced in positions of financial power by Keynesian-minded economists, industrialists, and labour leaders'.[84] The laissez-faire ideology of the pre-Second World War financial world was rejected by 'this new bloc of social forces', who were instead 'in favour of a more interventionist approach that would make the financial sector serve their broader economic and political objectives'.[85]

The move to curb finance was not altogether altruistic. The two chief negotiators at the conference, the US Treasury official Harry White and the British economist John Maynard Keynes, were both keenly aware that the need for social stability required curbs on capital.

In the words of Eric Helleiner:

In defending their Bretton Woods proposals, Keynes and White both outlined four central reasons why a liberal financial order was incompatible with the new welfare state. First, capital controls were needed to protect the new macroeconomic planning mechanisms developed in the 1930s from financial movements that were speculative and could cause disequilibrium in the system ... Second, as welfare expenditures grew, governments could no longer afford to allow their corporations and citizens to move funds abroad to evade taxes ... Finally, and most broadly, the welfare state had to be protected from flights of hot money induced by political reasons or a desire to influence legislation.[86]

The instability caused by the rampant financial speculation of the 1920s was incompatible with the adoption of the various government programmes in health, housing, welfare and employment that were key demands of citizens. In order for social democracy to thrive, there needed to be limits on the movement of capital. Governments needed corporations to keep their funds at home so as to shore up the national tax base to help fund these activities. Furthermore, the boom–bust extremities of employment and unemployment were to be avoided at all costs in order to avoid social revolution. National economic policy needed to lean towards full employment where possible. 'The plan accords to every member government the explicit right to control all capital movements,' said John Maynard Keynes, the chief negotiator for the British government. 'What used to be heresy is now endorsed as orthodox.'[87]

In terms of post-war Europe, the reconstruction was of a scale that capital could not be allowed to be hoarded or used for short-term profit. Governments therefore took a more direct role in the economic and social lives of citizens. The social contract that post-war Europe and the US demanded was incompatible with the business mechanisms of financial speculators. 'The bankers,' wrote Michael Moffitt in his book *The World's Money*, 'weakened politically and economically by the depression, finally accepted the agreement because they really had no alternative.'[88]

The post-war consensus in western democracies centred on social *and* economic development, and it strove for this through capital investments that were employment-heavy – in manufacturing and in social services such as health, education, housing and transport. The delegates at Bretton Woods believed that capitalism had gone too far; it needed to be saved *from itself*, otherwise the rest of Europe could follow the example of the Soviet Union or Nazi Germany. This was the main fear that drove Keynes and White. Indeed, Keynes' plans 'for a post-World War II clearing bank and international trade organisation was an attempt to understand the mechanisms that tend to turn liberal capitalism into a casino and thus to devise a means to protect the "physiological equilibrium" on which social order depends'.[89] The casino element, of course, is central to capitalist accumulation – capital begets capital – and is the reason why capitalism's so-called 'free markets' are an incredibly inefficient allocation of human and natural resources, as the focus is on the return to capital, not the return to society. Such misallocation leads to unemployment, poverty, inequality, social unrest and – if left unchecked – revolution.

The role of the state in the post-Second World War period was to address these socially unstable levels of underallocated and misallocated investment with the state providing a radical remedy of this condition through direct investment in socially necessary structures, such as housing, health, transport and education, in order to address the demands of citizens and organised labour. 'A class compromise between capital and labour was generally advocated as the key guarantor of domestic peace and tranquillity,' wrote David Harvey, and states 'actively intervened in industrial policy and moved to set standards for the social wage by constructing a variety of welfare systems'.[90] The international curbs on capitalist speculative investment as outlined in the Bretton Woods Agreement were designed to facilitate these more equitable – and socially stable – forms of investment.

But capitalism is what it is; it can no more curb its desire to accumulate more of itself than the fabled scorpion can curb its desire to sting the frog.[91] In the 1950s and 1960s it designed – with help from various states such as the US and UK – an alternative financial and banking system that operated for the most part outside the purview of regulators.

> *... they are particularly suitable for being used for speculative and arbitrage transactions of a disturbing kind.*
>
> Paul Einzig, September 1961[92]

As the 1950s progressed the supply of dollars worldwide increased as a result of the currency's role, under the Bretton Woods Agreement, as the basis for international exchange rates and payments. A significant amount of the excess dollars in Europe ended up on deposit with banks in Europe rather than on deposit with US-domiciled banks, as would normally have been the case. The growth of these European-domiciled dollar surpluses added to a market that was completely unregulated. In 1960 the Federal Reserve Bank of New York undertook an investigation into what it called the 'continental dollar market' and estimated that it exceeded '$1 billion, excluding any double counting for inter-bank deposits'.[93] It found that the dollar balances had been supplied 'mainly by Dutch, Swiss, Scandinavian and at times German banks, who may be joined by European central banks and by holders in the Middle East and south Asia', and that demand for euro-dollars (dollars on deposit in European banks) came mainly from 'Italian, French, British and Canadian banks, and recently from German and Japanese banks, as well as from branches of United States banks abroad'.[94]

By 1963 the euro-dollar market was causing significant trouble for the US balance of payments. The US Congress sub-committee on international exchange and payments heard evidence that 'US corporations have placed time deposits denominated in US dollars with the Canadian chartered banks, to the amount of over $400 million' and that part of that money ended up in the London euro-dollar market.[95] This was a direct drain on the US dollar reserves, and the type of activity that Bretton Woods had been designed to prevent. The US government responded with the Interest Equalization Tax, which was introduced in order to discourage investment in foreign securities and encourage investment in domestic securities. Instead, the restrictions led to a boom in euro-dollar transactions and the creation of a new bond in London that was denominated in the euro-dollar.

Despite the Bretton Woods system being circumvented so easily, no coordinated action was taken to ban the euro-dollar. In fact, this new and entirely unregulated market was given tacit support by both the US and UK governments. As Eric Helleiner points out in his 1994 publication *States and the Reemergence of Global Finance*, 'Britain provided a physical location for the market, permitting it to operate in London free of regulation', while 'by the mid-1960s, US officials were actively encouraging American banks and corporations to move their operations to the offshore London market'.[96] The euro-dollar market seemed to give both countries a way of placating the demands of finance while facilitating productive growth and high employment within their respective borders. In the case of Britain, 'it represented a solution to the problem of how to reconcile the goal of restoring London's international position within the Keynesian welfare state and Britain's deteriorating economic position'.[97] In the US 'the Johnson administration overtly encouraged [corporations] to use the Euromarket to finance their overseas operations, in order to discourage their opposition' to the various capital control programmes brought in to tackle the US balance of payments deficit.[98] 'US banks continued to finance the foreign activities of their corporate clients,' wrote Moffitt, 'they just did their lending from London.'[99]

By the late 1960s the euro-dollar market was estimated to stand at \$10 billion, all of it unregulated.[100] Moreover, the nature of the euro-dollar made it susceptible to speculators. 'Gratifying as this progress towards an increasing internationalisation of the monetary system may appear,' wrote the economist Paul Einzig in 1961, 'a close examination of the dynamic aspects of the new practice leads to some highly perturbing conclusions.'[101]

> The amounts involved – which are large and are increasing steadily – are held in a particularly loose and liquid form, and by their nature they are particularly suitable for being used for speculative and arbitrage transactions of a disturbing kind. Operations in Euro-dollars and similar deposits, instead of producing an equalising effect, are apt to produce in given circumstances exactly the opposite effect ... [The euro-dollar market] enables banks to expand credit over prolonged periods beyond the limit deemed advisable by the authorities.[102]

Less than fifteen years after the signing of the Bretton Woods Agreement, the unrestrained credit creation and speculative investment which that agreement had sought to curb was once again on the rise. Furthermore, this new credit was increasingly being used to fund *financial* speculation rather productive (that is, jobs-led) growth. It was not long until such instability began to manifest itself in the currency exchange system. The US trade deficit and the costs of the Vietnam War added to this instability. On 15 August 1971 the US suspended the convertibility of dollars into gold (a core feature of the Bretton Woods system) in what became known as the 'Nixon Shock'. The pound sterling broke from the dollar in July 1972. One month later, on 15 August, the US Treasury suspended all sales and purchases of gold. In March 1973 the then six members of the EEC agreed to break from the dollar and float their currencies. The Bretton Woods system had come to an end. By this stage the Eurocurrency market was estimated to stand at $132 billion, 'from a net size of some $8 billion in 1964'.[103]

The effective end of the Bretton Woods system was followed by a formal lifting of restrictions on international capital movements, first by Canada, Germany and Switzerland in 1973, and then by the US in 1974. This was followed by Britain in 1979, 'Japan in 1980, France and Italy in 1990, and Spain and Portugal in 1992'.[104] Debt had become the world's single largest tradeable commodity, pushed on developing countries as a Trojan horse for rent extraction and lobbed like cluster bombs into assets markets for the purposes of price speculation. 'The sheer scale and speed of these flows,' wrote John Eatwell and Lance Taylor in *Global Finance at Risk*, 'produced a succession of major financial crises [including] Latin America's Southern Cone crisis of 1979–81, the developing country debt crisis of 1982, the Mexican crisis of 1994–95, the Asian crisis of 1997–98, the Russian crisis of 1998, and the Brazilian crisis of 1999.'[105] In 2011 the US Financial Crisis Inquiry Commission found that with regard to the 2008 crisis, 'more than thirty years of deregulation and reliance on self-regulation by financial institutions, championed by former Federal Reserve chairman, Alan Greenspan and others, supported by successive administrations and Congresses, and actively pushed by the powerful financial industry at every turn, had stripped away key safeguards, which could have helped avoid catastrophe'.[106] The instability that Keynes and White tried to prevent with Bretton Woods was back with a vengeance.

The re-emergence of finance as a global force in the 1960s, the breakdown of the Bretton Woods Agreement in the 1970s, the sustained liberalisation of speculative capital flows in the 1980s and 1990s, and the current dazzling array of financial investment instruments such as derivatives and credit default swaps is commonly referred to as the 'financialisation' of the world economy. This was defined by the economist Gerald Epstein as 'the increasing role of financial motives, financial markets, financial actors and financial institutions in the operation of the domestic and international economies'.[107] In other words, it is the return of private capital interests to the centre stage of governmental economic and political policy in places such as Europe and the US, unburdened by the post-Second World War restraints of the social contract. More specifically, it is 'a pattern of accumulation in which profits accrue primarily through financial channels rather than through trade and commodity production', with 'financial' defined as 'activities relating to the provision (or transfer) of liquid capital in expectation of future interest, dividends, or capital gains'.[108]

Put simply, it is the pursuit of profit from paper assets, rather than actual production, which is at the heart of financialisation. This can include, for example, the transformation via a mortgage of an actual physical product such as a house into a paper asset. It is also seen in the increase of the so-called FIRE (Finance, Insurance and Real Estate) services in relation to the measurement of national output, despite their relatively low employment rates. The voices within these sectors – the lawyers, accountants, stockbrokers and estate agents, the administrators of paper claims – have been the most vocal in extolling the benefits of this merry dance with paper.

The dismantling of the gains commonly referred to as the welfare state was part of a conscious strategy by finance capital. It needed to weaken organised labour and the social supports provided by the state and paid for through general taxation in order to retain as much of the profit from investment for itself. Neoliberalism is the name given to this political project, although it has become such a negative term that it has probably lost the power to explain the world that, paradoxically, it now helps to define. In the words of the American scholar Stanley Fish, neoliberalism 'is a pejorative way of referring to a set of economic/political policies based on a strong faith in the beneficent effects of free markets'.[109] The Australian economist John Quiggin takes a similar view, calling it 'a poorly defined pejorative' for a system of thought and action that 'places much more weight on economic freedom than on personal freedom or civil liberties, reversing the emphasis of classical liberalism'.[110]

Despite these 'echo chamber' qualities, neoliberalism remains a useful shorthand. It has been best defined by David Harvey, who sees it as 'a political project carried out by the corporate capitalist class as they felt intensely threatened both politically and economically towards the end of the 1960s into the 1970s. They desperately wanted to launch a political project that would curb the power of labor.'[111] The rise of neoliberalism in the 1970s, therefore, was a kind of counter-revolution, a response to the rise of mass labour movements and the concessions wrung from business interests via trade union-influenced government policy. It also saw the expansion of the international system of tax havens, which today serve all major financial and commercial centres and are organised into three groups:

First and still by far the largest is made up of the UK-based or British Empire-based tax havens. Centred on the City of London and fed by the Euromarket, it consists of the Crown Dependencies, overseas territories, Pacific atolls, Singapore and Hong Kong.

The second consists of European Havens, specializing in headquarter centres, financial affiliates, and private banking. The third consists of a disparate group of either emulators, such as Panama, Uruguay, and Dubai, or new havens from the transition economies and Africa.[112]

The recent scandal of the Paradise Papers[113] brought home the extent of this alternative – and largely unregulated – system of offshore investment and tax avoidance, and as we will see in the next chapter, the Irish state is very much part of this system.

CONCLUSION

Money is a social technology, an indispensable tool of complex human societies. It is a way of mobilising resources and, left unchecked, it has the ability to concentrate social value in the hands of a few, even though such value is created through the actions of many. Its origins are in social and financial credit and debt obligations. The logic of money and the money system is a societal logic; it changes as society changes. The world we live in today is a capitalist world, and the money system reflects this reality.

The logic of capitalism is self-expansion – capital begets capital. 'What makes [a society] capitalist is not its predisposition to invest in a particular commodity (for example labour-power) or sphere of activity (for example, industry)', wrote the historian Giovanni Arrighi, a society 'is capitalist in virtue of the fact that its money is endowed with the "power of breeding" (Marx's expression) systemically and persistently, regardless of the particular commodities and activities that are incidentally the medium at any given time'.[114] Capitalism is about the accumulation of capital, and it does this by bringing into the money system those elements of human society and nature it believes will deliver a monetary return on its investment. It is a coercive system, built on violence, and one that requires a functioning state in order to operate. It was the merging of the state and capitalism in the seventeenth century – as exemplified by the foundation of the Bank of England – which finally gave capitalism the stability it needed to protect itself from itself.

By the second quarter of the twentieth century, however, this stability proved not only elusive but practically non-existent. The delegates at the Bretton Woods Conference worked on a plan for a global financial and trade system that would ameliorate the destabilising effects of capitalism, which searches for the greatest yield regardless of the social cost. War, collapse and revolution, as well as the growing strength of trade unions and working-class political parties, saw direct curbs on capitalism as well as significant, targeted investment in social services by governments across western democracies. Capitalism, however, regrouped and in the 1970s launched a counter-offensive known as neoliberalism. This was successful, resulting in seemingly permanent austerity, increasing inequality and widespread social and political unrest.

There are alternatives, but for them to have any chance of success there has to be an acceptance that money today is fused completely with the capitalist system. It is a fool's errand to believe that alternatives to the money system are viable when the logic of the money system is not in the gift of the money system but in the dominant societal logic – in our case, capitalism.

In terms of Ireland, this means looking at the relationship between Ireland and the global financial system, in particular at the international network of offshore financial centres and tax havens, of which Ireland is a key hub. It also means looking at the Irish elites who are gatekeepers for the money system in Ireland, as those elites will resist any change to the status quo. Significantly, they have the state on their side as well.

Ireland

INTRODUCTION

A key argument of this book is that money cannot be separated from the society in which it operates. It is not a thing that can be changed, like the wheels on a car, and for this reason I will not be putting forward alternatives to the *form* that money takes, such as bitcoin or local exchange trading systems (LETS), as I believe to do so is to entirely miss the point.[115] Money is an activity. It is part and parcel of an ongoing social, political and institutional dynamic. It shapes, and is shaped by, the world it inhabits, one that requires a legal framework and a coercive apparatus in the form of the state in order to operate.

The state, therefore, is key to money. The purpose of this chapter is to look at how money operates in Ireland and how it has shaped the history of the state, its institutions and its dominant political ideology. The reason for doing this will become clear in Chapter 3 when we look at organisational strategies for progressive change in

Ireland. The previous chapter talked of money in terms of political and economic power. The next chapter will talk of how to confront the political and economic power of money in Ireland. This chapter is the bridge between them. It will sketch the relationship between money and Irish political and economic institutions in order to help us build strategies to confront the inequalities caused by money and the money system in Ireland today.

Ireland is not closed to the rest of the world. Its money system is both national and international as exemplified by the currency it uses, the euro. It is also a tax haven and a hub in a global network of offshore financial centres.[116] This is not by accident; in fact, it is national state policy. Ireland has shaped its monetary policy and tax laws to serve the international monetary system and has spent decades building up the International Financial Services Centre (IFSC) as the 'jewel in the crown' of its strategy of foreign direct investment (FDI).

The Irish state accommodates the needs of local and foreign moneyed interests to the detriment of social cohesion and stability. Those local moneyed interests hawk the right of an independent state to set its own laws and tax policy. The mature Irish democracy, with its legal system that is recognised by international law, is traded by this class for the private gain of its privileged players. It is strongest within accountancy, stockbroking, banking, construction and the legal profession, as well as within the bureaucratic institutions of the state such as the Department of Finance, the Central Bank, and the Office of An Taoiseach. The interests of those engaged in facilitating national and international tax avoidance and loose monetary and financial regulation supersede the interests of ordinary citizens.

By way of example we have the story of Ireland and Apple, the American multinational. On 30 August 2016 an EU Commission investigation found that Ireland had breached state aid procedures by deliberately and artificially lowering the corporate tax rate paid by Apple.[117] Commissioner Margrethe Vestager, who headed the investigation, said that two separate rulings by the Irish Revenue Commissioners in 1991 and 2007 allowed Apple to be taxed in a way that 'did not correspond to economic reality'.[118] She concluded that the company paid an effective corporate tax rate of between 1 and 0.005 per cent on its European profits.[119]

Any tax ruling that benefits a company over its competitors is deemed to be illegal state aid under EU law. As such, the foregone tax liability for the years covering 2003 to 2014, estimated at €13 billion plus interest, would now have to be paid by Apple and collected by Ireland. The commission can only order recovery for the ten-year period preceding the start of its investigation, meaning that any outstanding tax due from 1991 to 2002 was outside of its legal remit.

The Irish state, which had recently exited from a Troika bailout programme and was still suffering from almost a decade of austerity cuts, rejected the finding and the €13 billion. The BBC commented that the Irish government's position 'seems odd in light of Ireland's recent history of economic trouble ... so why doesn't

Ireland want such a huge cash windfall?'[120] 'Ireland does not do deals with taxpayers,' the Department of Finance said in a press statement issued the day of the ruling.[121] 'Ireland acknowledges and accepts that the European Commission has a legitimate role, under the Treaties, in enforcing competition rules,' said the Department. However, in its view, it is 'not appropriate that EU State aid competition rules are being used in this new and unprecedented way in the area of taxation, which is a Member State competence and a fundamental matter of sovereignty'.[122] Michael Noonan, the Irish Minister for Finance, told journalists to 'look at the small print on an Apple iPhone, it says designed in California and manufactured in China and that means any profits that accrued didn't accrue in Ireland and so I can't see why the tax liability is in Ireland'.[123]

Unfortunately for Minister Noonan and Apple, the EU Commission did not base its investigation on the small print etched on the back of an iPhone but on the balance sheets, board meetings, company structure and booked sales of Apple Sales International and Apple Operations Europe, two Irish-based companies that utilised a cost-sharing agreement with their US parent, Apple Inc., for tax avoidance purposes.

The arrangement was in place until the companies changed their structures in 2015 due to the fallout from the 2013 US Senate Permanent Subcommittee on Investigations inquiry into Apple.[124] The chair of the subcommittee, Senator Carl Levin, found that Apple 'quietly negotiated with the Irish Government an income tax rate of less than two percent [and] in practice, Apple is able to pay a rate far below even that low figure'.[125] This led Levin to conclude that 'Apple used cost-sharing arrangements that it has with offshore subsidiaries to shift income from the United States to Ireland, an effective tax haven, where it pays effectively no taxes at all'.[126] The EU Commission investigation was a direct result of the evidence uncovered at those hearings.

The concept of a tax ruling constituting illegal state aid is a long-established one in the EU. The Apple case may have been unusual given the size of the liability, but not in judgement. Article 107 of the Treaty of the Functioning of the European Union (TFEU) outlines a general block on state aid and is itself based on one of the founding articles of the 1957 Treaty of Rome. There are exceptions, including aids that have a social character, but in general an enterprise is seen to have received state aid 'if it is relieved from charges normally borne by similar firms'.[127]

The European Court of Justice has consistently ruled that tax exemptions for individual enterprises constitute a relief from normal charges. It found, in 1994, in a judgement against the Spanish state, that 'a measure by which the public authorities grant to certain undertakings a tax exemption which, although not involving a transfer of State resources, places the persons to whom the tax exemption applies in a more favourable financial situation than other taxpayers constitutes State aid'.[128] This ruling is an established piece of EU case law.[129] Despite decades of citation, Minister Noonan and his mandarins in the Department of Finance were shocked in 2016 to find that favourable tax rulings for individual firms may be classified as illegal.

One week after the commission's report, the Dáil was recalled from its summer recess to debate a motion on the ruling. The government had decided to appeal, and the reasons for its decision were outlined in an explanatory memorandum that had been given to all members of the Oireachtas. The action was necessary, it said, in order 'to defend the integrity of our tax system, to provide tax certainty to business, and to challenge the encroachment of EU state aid rules into the sovereign Member State competence of taxation'.[130] The Taoiseach and leader of Fine Gael, Enda Kenny, told the House that the finding was wrong and 'cannot be allowed to stand'.[131] 'As the Government has made clear,' he said, 'we will appeal it before the European courts with every expectation of success.'

Minister Noonan said that the appeal 'is not in any way an endorsement of aggressive tax planning arrangements, nor is it a defence of the extremely low effective tax rates that can be achieved under the broken international tax system'. 'We clearly compete for foreign direct investment,' he said, 'but do so from a position of legitimacy. Our tax corporation code is founded on fairness, transparency, consistency and the rule of law.'

Micheál Martin, leader of Fianna Fáil, fully backed the government's position. 'The attempt to paint Ireland as a rogue nation on tax has been ongoing for decades,' he said. 'It has been in place since well before any of the measures attacked by the Commission existed and before many of our largest firms even existed.' He ended by saying that the 'risk to Ireland is simply too big to ignore. We must fight this judgement by every means possible.'

The Labour Party also supported the appeal. 'Having known and worked with the Irish Revenue Commissioners for three decades,' said the party's leader Brendan Howlin, 'I, for one, accept their word on these matters.' His party colleague Alan Kelly said that the ruling was 'an effort to go after our country and our corporation tax rate through the back door', while the former party leader Joan Burton stated that the issue was one of jealousy. 'Ireland has a tax regime that is attractive to foreign investors,' she said, 'and it is the envy of some of our larger neighbours. Let us not be guileless about that.'

Ninety-three TDs voted to reject the €13 billion windfall, thirty-six voted to accept it. It was a decision that also divided public opinion.[132]

For all the high talk of defending Ireland, taking on Europe and protecting the honour of the Revenue Commissioners, the actual energy behind the government's rejection of €13 billion in much-needed revenue was a lot more prosaic. Despite official claims to the contrary, Ireland is a tax haven for transnational capital. An indigenous class of lawyers, economists, accountants, lobbyists and legislators has built up over the decades to facilitate and support this network. In 1987 Ireland set up the IFSC. It marked a dramatic shift in industrial policy, with the state increasingly focusing on tax law trickery over actual investment as the core of its FDI strategy. The Socialist Party TD Paul Murphy made this very point during the Dáil debate on Apple. 'The Government,' he said, 'supported by Fianna Fáil and Labour, is waging a fight with public money to defend the right of one of the biggest companies in the world to pay no tax. It is as simple as that.'

The majority of companies in Ireland – both Irish and foreign-owned – pay little or no corporate tax. In 2014, 68 per cent of all companies liable for the tax paid nothing.[133] In 2000 the figure was 48 per cent.[134] The narrowing of the tax base means that the burden of paying for the running of the state, as well as meeting the interest repayments due on the bank bailout loans, falls more and more on ordinary working people and their families. This has significant consequences in terms of social cohesion and state viability, as can be seen in the ongoing funding crises in health, housing, education and infrastructure.

The Tax Justice Network[135] estimated that in 2012 somewhere between \$21 to \$32 trillion was hidden in offshore centres across the globe.[136] This is the system that the Irish state protects. It does so because the interests of a significant part of its moneyed class are dependent on its survival, despite the damage it inflicts on Irish society, and that class has not only the ear of the state, but has seen to it that the interests of the state's financial and monetary institutions are prioritised above all others. Discussions on bitcoin and local trading systems would not challenge this class in any way. In order to effect real change in Ireland in terms of how money operates and in whose interest, at the very least the institutions of the state need to be reformed. For that to happen, we need to understand how they came to be the way they are. That requires an historical investigation.

> *[Saorstát Éireann] is now, and will undoubtedly long continue to be, an integral part of the economic system at the head of which stands Great Britain ...*
> Irish Banking Commission, 1927 [137]

On 16 January 1922, the chairman of the Irish provisional government, Michael Collins, stood in the courtyard of Dublin Castle and formally took charge of Saorstát Éireann (the Irish Free State). A story is told that when he arrived the Lord Lieutenant of Ireland, Viceroy Fitzalan, said to him, 'You are seven minutes late, Mr Collins', to which Collins replied, 'We've been waiting over 700 years, you can have the extra seven minutes.'[138] The story, which is almost certainly apocryphal, nonetheless speaks to the official interpretation of Ireland's partitioned independence: that the political break with Westminster effectively ended Britain's role in the affairs of the Free State and that independence after a centuries-old struggle was finally won. The reality, as always, is a little more mundane.

The Dublin Castle handover of power did not include the money system. The Irish Free State remained part of the sterling area, with the Bank of England as its central bank and monetary policy effectively set by London.

Political union may have been severed, but financial union remained. This was an outcome that the provisional Irish government wanted. The Irish banking system was entirely focused on the London financial markets and was in no mind to change its position; the provisional government concurred. Both were resistant to the development of an Irish currency subject to democratic oversight. The Irish banking system was also against any kind of state-led credit formation to address the infrastructural demands of the state, as it saw credit as its own preserve, not that of the state.

The Irish Free State also remained part of the UK economy. Its role within that economy was primarily agricultural, more specifically, the provision of livestock for the finishing farms and slaughterhouses of England. This relationship, not surprisingly, benefited livestock breeders and traders, who had come to prominence in the post-Famine era when land was cleared and secured for grazing rather than tillage. This became a source of conflict within Irish rural society, between small farmers and graziers, as seen by the 'ranch wars' of the early twentieth century in the midlands and the west of Ireland, where 'cattle drives, the destruction of property and the boycott of local farmers and their families formed part of a web of rural intimidation aimed at petty landlords and grazing farmers'.[139] Upon independence, however, it was the graziers who were in the ascent and Irish economic policy developed with their interests very much at heart. 'The primacy of agriculture was enshrined as the government accepted that the economy depended on it for prosperity, that agricultural prosperity depended on the export market, that that market essentially comprised of Britain, and that the most profitable Irish product in Britain was cattle.'[140] The Free State was politically an independent country but still tied to Britain through agriculture and finance.

In terms of the economy, the government's plan to keep economic and monetary policies as they were pre-independence ignored the obvious fact that things were not the same anymore. The island had been partitioned into two separate political entities, with the twenty-six-county Free State now responsible for its own political affairs. Yet, the approach of the government was to behave as if Ireland remained a regional economy within the UK. In real terms, this meant the continuation of trade in livestock and finance. The three government-appointed commissions set up to examine the economy – the Commission on Agriculture (1924), the Fiscal Inquiry Committee (1923) and the Banking Commission (1927) – all decided in their majority reports that things should remain as they were, that 'Ireland would maintain parity and financial links with sterling, produce food for Britain, and retain a free-trade industrial sector'.[141]

The problem with this approach was that the type of central government fiscal transfers and shared costs which regions could expect as part of a greater national economy such as the UK were now all but gone – for example, the public housing projects initiated after the Great War but from which Saorstát Éireann was excluded, as well as government funding for primary education. Ireland was now a nation-state and needed to fund these projects itself, but instead of working towards the creation of a national economy with an independent fiscal policy and actual agricultural products for export (not just livestock), the Irish government took to protecting the relatively small percentage of farmers, financiers and administrators who made a comfortable living from the deficiencies of the Irish economy, while consigning the rest of the population to poverty and emigration.

All government borrowing is either paid back or guaranteed by taxation. The resistance against borrowing is ultimately one against the increase in taxation that is necessary to pay for it. The Irish Free State was a low-tax economy and the local moneyed interests wanted to keep it that way. Yet the newly formed state needed targeted investment in social and industrial infrastructure if it was to develop as an independent state. Furthermore, it needed banks to reinvest Irish savings in the Irish economy. Instead, the banks effectively exported Irish savings to London where they were used to invest in the British economy instead of the Irish economy. The state was slowly being starved of credit at a time when it needed it most. The sad irony is that generations of Irish people ended up working in England on projects that were funded in part through Irish bank deposits while back home the country was falling apart for want of credit. As far as the state's institutions were concerned, this was all perfectly normal.

From 1923 to 1953 the Department of Finance was headed in turn by two arch-conservative figures: Joseph Brennan and J.J. McElligott. Both were products of the British civil service system and were instrumental in ensuring that Finance was the dominant government department, as the Treasury was in the UK. McElligott held the view, expressed in later life, that one positive outcome of the Irish civil war 'was that it enabled senior civil servants to construct the fabric of administrative government in the Free State without interference from the politicians'.[142] Both Brennan and McElligott held 'an aversion to the working class in general, and to organised labour in particular'.[143] Irish moneyed interests would not be threatened by independence.

One of the first acts of the new Irish state was to designate the privately owned Bank of Ireland as its financial agent. It took on this role on 19 January 1922, three days after the British authorities formally handed over power to the provisional government. William P. Cairnes, governor of the Bank of Ireland, said at the time that 'among the many serious problems which have to be solved there are two of special interest to us bankers, namely, currency and finance'.[144] He saw his role, and that of the Bank of Ireland, as ensuring that the financial objectives of the new state did not end up clashing with the needs of shareholders in Irish banks. 'I wish it to be known that any information, advice, or assistance in our power will most willingly and gladly be given when asked for,' he told the Bank's board of directors.[145] 'I am confident that in expressing this view I do not speak for the Bank of Ireland alone, but voice the unanimous opinion of the Irish banks.'[146] The Bank of Ireland was the government's bank until 1 January 1972, almost thirty years *after* the formation of the Irish Central Bank.

There were some issues that needed to be addressed, even for the arch-conservatives. Saorstát Éireann had no legal tender. Sterling notes and coins were used on a daily basis but there was pressure on the state as an independent country to have its own physical currency. On 3 February 1926 the Minister for Finance, Ernest Blythe, announced the establishment of a banking commission to consider issues surrounding the standard of value, legal tender, and the appointment and re-allocation of bank note issues.

The commission's members were drawn from banking and finance. It made a virtue of this, saying in its final report that 'our body included within its members several bankers of long and tried experience, thoroughly familiar with local conditions, in close touch with banking and financial interests, and hence able to assure us of the view of that element of the community'.[147] It went on to conclude that Saorstát Éireann 'is now, and will undoubtedly long continue to be, an integral part of the economic system at the head of which stands Great Britain [and] will undoubtedly continue for an indefinite period to find the great bulk of its market for exports in Great Britain'.[148] It was the official economic and monetary policy of the Irish state that it remain within the sterling area, with the UK as its dominant trading partner.

The report's one concession to change was a recommendation for a Currency Commission, the remit of which would be the oversight of the physical production and maintenance of a new currency which 'shall be stated in terms of sterling, thus accepting the British standard of Value ... and it shall be convertible at par into British sterling'.[149] Credit formation, allocation and general monetary policy would stay the same, that is, in the hands of the Bank of England, the private banks, and a deferential Department of Finance.

The election of Fianna Fáil to government in 1932 saw no real change in monetary policy, despite the fact that it had previously called for the creation of an Irish central bank and a greater role for government in credit formation and capital investment. The party's leader, Éamon de Valera, said in January 1929 that one of the first acts of a Fianna Fáil government 'would be to repeal the Currency Act and place the control of the Free State currency and credit in the hands of Irishmen, instead of in the hands of the Bank of England and, through that institution, in the hands of the British government'.[150] Once in power, though, the party moved away from this position. Indeed, the party's Finance Minister, Seán McEntee, completely embraced the 'Merrion Street orthodoxy' of the Department of Finance.[151] He sought and received advice from three main sources: the secretary of the department, J.J. McElligott, the chairman of the Currency Commission, Joseph Brennan, and the chairman of the Irish Banks' Standing Committee.[152]

The 1930s, however, was a period of global economic and political crisis, one that saw a re-evaluation internationally of the role of governments and central banks in monetary policy. The Irish state belatedly responded to these moves when, on 26 October 1934, Minister McEntee announced the appointment of a commission to inquire into banking, currency and related matters. It was tasked with examining the system of 'currency, banking credit, public borrowing and lending and the pledging of State credit on behalf of agriculture, industry and social services'.[153] Furthermore, and in a departure from the previous commission, it would actively 'consider and report what changes, if any, are necessary or desirable to promote the social and economic welfare of the community and the interests of agriculture and industry'. Its majority report, published in October 1938, found that while a central bank should now be established, parity with sterling should also be maintained, and government borrowing should be curtailed. It also rejected the idea of a nationalised bank to provide credit for national investment. In other words, it recommended the retention of the status quo, save for some minor concessions to the establishment of a central bank.

The commission also produced a minority report, signed by Professor Alfred O'Rahilly of University College Cork, and two trade unionists, William O'Brien and Seán Campbell. 'The political union [with Britain] ceased in 1922,' they wrote, 'but the financial union still persists, accompanied by the benediction of most of our economists.'[154] They said that the 'British authorities look after their own interests, real or supposed; and we fall into line, not after careful investigation of our own interests, but automatically because ... we have subordinated our domestic currency policy to the views of the British'.[155] In their view:

No case whatever has been made out to show that a continuation of our present anomalous financial system will ever solve our major social problems. Nor can we see why ... we should be asked to tighten our belts in order to preserve the relics of a political union which our people have vigorously severed.

As far as financial unionism is concerned, it has been preserved intact in spite of some quite superficial green-painting involving nothing more than a modest revenue to the state. The bankers, being practical men, have gone on as before, continuing to deal with the essentially unchanged reality.

We have the utmost sympathy with the plea that we should proceed cautiously and gradually, that we should allay all reasonable suspicions and doubts. But we cannot acquiesce in the extraordinary view that this country, alone among the political responsible entities in the world, should not even have the power to make decisions, that no apparatus or mechanism for controlling the volume and direction of credit should ever be brought into existence.[156]

In conclusion, they said that 'we need an organ for the issue and control of developmental credit. This is our fundamental conclusion; and the only thing startling about it is that it was not accepted sixteen years ago.'[157]

The authors of the minority report noted that while their colleagues on the Banking Commission 'exhaustively examined and reported on the system of currency, banking, credit etc.', they in response had confined themselves to what they saw as the core objective of the commission, that is, to recommended what they considered 'the fundamental change which we consider necessary and desirable to promote the social and economic welfare of the community and the interests of agriculture and industry'.[158] Given the ideological and moneyed interests of Irish banks and the Department of Finance, it is no wonder such objectives were utterly rejected.

Five years after publication of the report and with severely limited powers, an Irish central bank was finally established on 29 January 1943. The characteristic functions of a central bank were not assigned to it. The bank did not acquire the cash reserves of the commercial banks. It was not designated as government banker, that role was kept, as already stated, by the Bank of Ireland until 1972. It had no statutory power to restrict credit, and in the absence of a domestic money market 'the conditions for influencing credit by open-market operations did not exist'.[159] The first governor of the bank was Joseph Brennan, a safe pair of hands as far as the establishment was concerned. Ireland's monetary policy was predicated on the continued global dominance

of the sterling area, as had been the case since 1922. The
Second World War, however, put paid to that.

One of the consequences of the post-war Bretton
Woods Agreement was the slow break-up of the sterling area.[160] This posed something of a dilemma for the
Irish state as its entire monetary policy was predicated
on sterling's global position. Decades of underinvest-
ment that was due, in part, to the export of Irish bank
deposits (and Irish credit) for investment in London's
financial markets meant that Ireland found itself having
to modernise but without any of the monetary tools to
do so. Now was the time to invest and to give the Irish
Central Bank and Department of Finance the powers
they needed, but this would have meant removing the
hold that the banks had on the supply and direction
of investment, as well as breaking the parity link with
sterling. The Irish state was not willing to do either.

At this point we need to return briefly to the
importance of money and investment to a society. One
of the issues the Bretton Woods Agreement tried to
address was the rampant misallocation of capital (money
as investment) in the decades leading up to the Great
Depression and Second World War. From 1922 onwards,
the Irish state was no different. It kept itself out of
monetary policy – leaving it to the Bank of England –
and allowed the private banks to direct investment for
the benefit of their respective shareholders, not for the
needs of Irish society in general. This saw Irish banks
continue to invest in the financial markets in London – a
policy facilitated by the parity between sterling and the

Irish pound – rather than buying Irish government debt or providing reasonable interest rates at home to make capital investment loans affordable for farmers and businesses. Starved of credit, Irish business and agricultural sectors floundered. They could not afford to invest in themselves as Irish bank interest rates and the link with sterling made bank credit unaffordable for all but the most secure of businesses.

In other words, the peculiar dynamics of Irish monetary policy and private bank credit allocation were a structural problem within the Irish economy – and by structural, I mean they had an institutional and legal form. These peculiarities existed to benefit Irish banks and their long-standing practice of investing in London's financial markets rather than at home, but they also benefited the arch-conservatives within the permanent state and political parties who saw the maintenance of the link with sterling as a means to keep public expenditure and taxation down. When it comes to using a currency as a means to implement austerity, Ireland was a pioneer in the field. War and the Bretton Woods Agreement, though, changed the international monetary landscape, and the Irish state needed to adapt.

Where do we find dollars?
Irish Times, 26 June 1948[161]

Europe was in desperate need of reconstruction following the devastation of the war. One of the problems it faced related to funding for capital investment and in response to this the US State Department initiated in 1947 the European Recovery Program, also known as the Marshall Aid Plan. It marked a dramatic shift in global power and influence. Its dual purpose was to combat the spread of communism in Europe and secure raw materials and markets for US capital. It was, in essence, a policy 'to remake the old world in the image of the new'.[162] The US undersecretary of state for economic affairs, Will Clayton, told a departmental meeting in May 1947 that while the initiative behind the Marshall Plan should 'come – or at any rate, appear to come – from Europe … the United States must run the show. And it must start running it now'.[163] Britain saw things differently. It had survived the Blitz. It had won the war. It still had an empire. It was a highly indebted nation but with the financial network of the City of London and sterling as a global currency it had every intention of getting back on its feet. The problems were credit, its outstanding US loans and dollar convertibility.

The Marshall Aid Plan meant that Britain was not able to freely convert sterling to dollars to address any trade deficit. It had to 'earn' its dollars through trade. And Ireland, which had used the City of London to purchase dollars in the past, now had to do the same; Ireland had to trade goods and services with the US in order to get the dollars it needed to purchase American goods and also pay back its Marshall aid loans.[164] 'Ireland's main contribution to European recovery will take place through the production of more food for export,' said the US State Department.[165] 'To expand its exports of agricultural products,' it added, 'Ireland needs to mechanise its agriculture, obtain more fertilisers and animal feed-stuffs, increase its imports of fuel and overhaul its transportation system.'[166] This meant that Ireland had to move away from its essentially mono-line trade link with Britain (cattle), and towards making its own goods and selling them to other countries, including the US. This meant capital investment in infrastructure and industry, something to which the Department of Finance and the Irish Central Bank were implacably opposed.

In March 1947 the Central Bank of Ireland argued against capital investment in infrastructure and other productivity measures. 'It is important as a safeguard against inflation that the monetary reactions of projected large schemes should be carefully studied,' it said in its annual report.[167] 'Production in the capital field cannot wisely be undertaken except in due proportion.'[168] The analysis put forward by the Irish Central Bank was completely out of step with reality. 'Inadequate capital investment has long characterised Irish agriculture and much of the capital equipment now in use suffered serious deterioration during the war,' said the US State Department.[169] 'As a result Ireland had in 1947 almost the lowest number of power units, including tractors, horses and other work animals per acre of arable land of any Organisation for European Economic Co-operation (OEEC) country.'[170] This was despite the fact that, according to the Irish Department for External Affairs, post-war Ireland was 'a creditor nation with large resources of capital and with ample manpower for development [and where] industrial production is low in relation to the consumption requirements and productive capacities of the country'.[171]

The blockage lay within the key institutions of Irish finance, namely the private banks, the Department of Finance and the Central Bank. While the Irish government recognised that the state needed to develop long-term sources of dollar earnings, it was also clear that it did not want to address monetary policy and financial investment shortcomings in the process, it did not want to tackle the deep-rooted and highly dysfunctional financial and economic power blocs within the state. As a result, Ireland missed the opportunity offered by the new markets of post-war Europe and of the OEEC, of which Ireland was a founder member. It remained focused on Britain and by the mid-1950s found itself in a death spiral of austerity and emigration. The need for indigenous investment, the breaking of the parity link with sterling, the widening of the tax net to include farmers and ranchers, and the establishment of a genuine central bank were all essential in order for the economy to develop, and all were fiercely resisted.

Out of this resistance a 'new way' was flagged, which was the expansion of the economy through foreign investment. This became the means of industrialisation for Ireland, one which avoided the need to expand the tax base, reform monetary policy, or in any way seriously challenge the status quo. Foreign direct investment started as a quick fix but morphed into a long-term industrial policy.[172]

By the mid-1980s job growth by way of FDI had stalled. The next idea was to extend Ireland's corporation tax rate to financial businesses. This was given a boost in 1987 when the leader of the opposition, Charles Haughey, announced a proposal to establish a low-tax zone for the international financial services in Ireland. The plan was to create a designated area within the state where qualifying companies would be able 'to undertake any business in the financial services area they choose and subject to new legislation specifically passed for the centre'.[173] In the election of that year, Haughey was returned as Taoiseach and one of his first acts was to establish a committee to offer advice on the financial services centre. It recommended that the government go ahead with its plans.

Almost from the start, the IFSC was used for tax avoidance. 'The Financial Centre is spawning other asset financing operations,' wrote the journal *Finance* in April 1988, 'essentially founded on the niche opportunity presented by the international tax arbitrage available in Ireland, and available through Custom House financial licences.'[174] Such practices, all given the silent nod by the regulators within the Irish Central Bank, were an early signal of things to come. By June 1991 the IFSC was dominated by asset finance, corporate treasury and captive insurance activities, with the majority of companies either from Ireland, Germany, the UK or the USA.[175]

The focus on tax avoidance led to a boost in business for indigenous Irish tax consultants. 'The policy of Irish governments over the past ten years or so of creating tax-based industry incentives has greatly contributed to the growth of tax practices,' wrote Kevin Warren, partner at Craig Gardner/Price Waterhouse, 'as clients need specific advice on the exploitation of these reliefs.'[176]

Not all were happy with the tax arbitrage of the IFSC. The German authorities in particular highlighted the volume of funds being invested by German fund managers through subsidiary companies in the centre. They saw such activity as merely a way of repatriating profits whilst avoiding German taxes. 'The net result,' wrote *Finance* magazine in September 1991, 'is that the German exchequer is suffering a massive loss of tax revenue.'[177] The Irish responded that the tax incentives that propped up the IFSC had already been approved by the EC as a way of addressing unemployment. The problem was that asset management was not a particularly labour-intensive activity. 'If you increase the level of funds you are managing,' said the manager of an IFSC-based German company, 'that does not mean you automatically need more people to manage them.'[178] The IFSC would continue to exhibit anaemic job growth until the late 1990s and the creation of the euro.

Ireland also offered investors a 'hands-off' regulatory environment. This was often a deciding factor for companies that set up an office in the IFSC. Mr Hiroshi Hayashi, president of Mitsubishi Trust and Banking Corporation, told *The Irish Times* in October 1990 that he was always 'on the lookout for places with as little regulation and as much tax incentive as possible from which to do business' and that this combination was the reason behind the bank's decision to locate in Ireland.[179] Dermot Desmond, one of the key architects of the IFSC proposal, said that in its opening year the Custom House Docks site had increased the need for a new regulatory structure which is both equitable and competitive'.[180] Brian Cregan, director of the Financial Services Industry Association, saw Ireland having 'a prudent regulatory structure conforming to the agreed European criteria without repeating the excesses of the UK'.[181] The Irish Minister for Finance, Albert Reynolds, told a seminar in Tokyo to promote the IFSC that the regulation of the centre 'is being achieved with commendable flexibility and without formal detailed rule books'.[182] The legal profession also benefited from the IFSC. Irish law firms actively assisted 'in the development of new products, as well as adapting existing ones to a new environment', with early legislation such as the 1990 Unit Trusts Act written with significant input from financial lawyers.[183] These three elements – backroom support services, loose regulation and an ultra-low tax rate – were brought together in a physical location in Dublin's docklands.

In August 1991 *The New York Times* ran a special report on offshore banking centres. It wrote that tax havens were no longer simply places full of 'tax-dodging rich people or crooks hiding ill-gotten gains' but rather facilitated 'international banks and corporations, seeking higher profits'.[184] 'They occupy a kind of shadowland of finance,' it said, with new entrants 'crowding the field'. Among them was Ireland, which had 'established the

International Financial Services Center [sic] three years ago as a tax haven in Dublin'.

By 2005 the IFSC was being referred to as 'the wild west of European finance'.[185] At the same time a litany of Irish politicians, journalists and financial experts spoke in glowing terms about the 'light touch' of the country's financial regulations and the necessity of a low corporation tax rate in order to keep the Celtic Tiger alive. An *Irish Times* editorial in August 2007 urged caution with regard to regulation. 'On the face of it, there appears to be a strong case for stricter regulation of international financial services here,' wrote the paper's editor. 'In considering any such action, however, it is important to have regard to the role that the existing "light touch" regulatory regime has played in the development of a world-class [Irish] financial services industry in a few short decades.'[186] The editorial perfectly captured the consensus on Ireland's loose regulations, tax haven measures, and absolute deference to all things financial.

> *... a battle over loss allocation.*
> Ed Kane, 28 January, 2015[187]

Before we move into the Irish bank crisis and what it showed us about the relationship between money, banking, politics and the state, we need to reflect once more on the nature of banking itself.

The standard description of a bank is that it is an institution licensed to take deposits and make loans, and which acts as an intermediary between borrowers and savers.[188] It gives the impression of the institution as a kind of economic matchmaker, helping those who have money to meet up with those who need money. However, there are two things to keep in mind. First of all, banks create credit when they make loans, and by doing so add to the volume of money in circulation.[189] Secondly, they have a significant influence over the *direction* of investment, in terms of consumption, industry, services and social infrastructure.

Banks *actively shape* the nature of investment, and this is driven not so much by the needs of a society but by the imperative of a bank to make a return for its shareholders. To go back to Bretton Woods, it was the misallocation of capital by banks that the agreement sought to address. Sometimes the needs of a society and a bank's shareholders coalesce; other times, they do not. Banks are not simply intermediaries. They are not the concierge of capitalism; they are a part of it, a crucial player in its overall dynamic and have been since the late middle ages and early modern period.

We can see this with regard to Ireland and its banks, in particular in relation to the 2008 crisis. I have covered the crisis in detail elsewhere,[190] but in general the years leading up to the guarantee saw the greatest misallocation of capital investment in the state's history, as Irish banks poured hundreds of billions of euros into commercial and residential property ventures at home and abroad over a five-year period from 2003 to 2008. This was encouraged by bank and developer-lobbied tax credit and planning policies that made commercial and residential property development a highly lucrative but increasingly precarious venture. In order to fund this lending, Irish banks increasingly relied on international money markets.

Towards the middle of 2007 these markets started to freeze up as the subprime mortgage crisis took hold in the US. This was at a time when Irish banks were fatally overexposed to property investment; for example, just twenty-nine developers had debts of at least €34 billion across the banking system, with significant levels of 100 per cent funding from certain institutions.[191] 'Few, if any, financial institutions wanted to be left out of what was seen as a profitable business due to larger lending margins and relatively low operating costs,' the chief executive of the National Asset Management Agency (NAMA) told the Oireachtas bank inquiry in 2015.[192] It had the effect of concentrating bank lending risk to a small number of Irish commercial property developers.

Despite the fact that commercial property was the crucial element in the collapse of the banks, mortgage-holders were routinely listed as the root cause of the problem. When the then Minister for Finance, Brian Lenihan, said on RTÉ's *Prime Time* in November 2010, 'Let's be fair about it: we all partied', he was referring to wage-workers and home purchasers, and not to those tied up with the speculative and securitised land-banks, hotels and office blocks that destroyed Anglo, Irish Nationwide and indeed the Irish banking system.[193]

The damage done by commercial property could be seen in NAMA where the government concentrated the riskiest part of Irish bank portfolios. This was highlighted by the EU Commission in February 2010, when it stated that 'the assets targeted by [NAMA] are all loans issued for the purchase, exploitation or development of land as well as loans either secured or guaranteed by land, and some of their associated commercial loans'.[194] There is no mention of a mortgage or residential crash. In the end, of the 230,000 permanently vacant housing units recorded in the 2011 state census, only 4,000 ended up in NAMA.[195]

The banks most exposed to commercial property were Anglo Irish Bank and Irish Nationwide, the two banks at the heart of the guarantee and subsequent bailout. In June 2012 Professor Karl Whelan of UCD Economics Department authored a report that highlighted the tightening of lending on the international capital markets in 2007 and 2008, which made it increasingly difficult for banks to roll over their funding. As a consequence of this, Irish banks 'began to borrow from the Eurosystem to pay off maturing bonds', he said, adding that 'when Anglo Irish Bank ran out of Eurosystem-eligible collateral in September 2008, the Irish government chose to offer a blanket guarantee to all depositors and the vast majority of bondholders in the domestic Irish banks'.[196]

Anglo Irish Bank was the institution most at risk of collapse and was guaranteed even though it was not of systemic importance to the Irish economy. In January 2009 the Department of Finance, in a report to the EU Commission, said that the bank operated within a 'niche market rather than [the] broad market'.[197] That niche was property speculation. On 15 January 2009 Brian Lenihan announced that Anglo Irish Bank would be placed under public ownership. The previous week the financial management and advisory company Merrill Lynch, in a report that cost the government €7.4 million, had said that the bank was 'fundamentally sound'.[198] 'The proposed Anglo nationalisation marks a decisive watershed in Irish democracy,' wrote Morgan Kelly. 'With it, an Irish government has coolly looked its citizens in the eye and said: "Sorry, but your priorities are not ours."'[199]

The Fianna Fáil/Green coalition government brought in three budgets in the wake of the banking crisis. Each one had a deflationary impact on the Irish economy. The first of these budgets was put to the Dáil on 14 October 2008, less than two weeks after the bank guarantee was signed into law. Normally, Irish budgets are put before the Dáil during the first week in December. Brian Lenihan said that the decision to move the budget forward by two months was made so that the government could 'seize the initiative [and provide] political leadership in the time of changed economic realities'.[200] He added that 'while the strength of the economy in the past decade has given us some room for manoeuvre, we cannot put our reputation for fiscal responsibility in jeopardy'. With this in mind, Lenihan told the Dáil that the government planned 'to reduce public expenditure as much as possible on the current side and as much as is sensible on the capital side'. Lenihan said that the choices made in the budget did not serve any vested interest. 'Rather,' he said, 'it provides an opportunity for us all to pull together and play our part according to our means so that we can secure the gains which have been the achievement of the men and women of this country.' He ended the speech by saying that the budget was 'no less than a call to patriotic action', thus proving that while patriotism may be the last refuge of a scoundrel, it's the first port of call for a government minister under pressure.

The debt obligations bestowed on the state by the banks and speculators, however, were impossible to bear. In May 2010 Greece was forced to accept EU/IMF funding in return for a series of austerity budgets. It was reckoned that either Ireland or Portugal was next. The pathological rush to deflate the Irish economy, the obvious instability of the Irish banking system, and the announcement that the government intended cutting a further €15 billion from its budget, saw the state slide towards its endgame.

On 18 November 2010 a delegation from the IMF and EU arrived in Dublin to discuss a funding strategy for Ireland, despite a deluge of almost surreal denials by the government that such meetings were even taking place. By the end of the week an announcement was made that Ireland had accepted a three-year, €85 billion euro, bailout. Ireland would contribute €17 billion from its national pension fund while the remaining €68 billion would come from the EU, the IMF, and individual states within the European Union. The news shook the ruling Fianna Fáil/Green coalition to its core, eventually leading to a general election in February 2011. Both government parties were decimated at the polling stations. The Taoiseach-in-waiting, Enda Kenny, assured the Irish public that he would not shirk from the 'tough choices' to be made regarding cuts in social provisions. He also promised that, above all else, Ireland's corporation tax rate would remain untouched. The parties may have changed but the approach from the state stayed the same: above all else, protect the banks and the tax avoidance system. Five years later this attitude was endorsed once again by the government in the case of Apple and the €13 billion in lost revenue.

CONCLUSION

The 2008 banking crisis was not caused by an outbreak of moral failure or the result of individual weakness. The significant power of Irish banks to dictate economic and monetary policies, and to protect themselves against the negative consequences of such policies, had developed over decades and runs deep within Irish society. The decision by the government to guarantee the deposits and liabilities of the Irish banks was the money system *acting as a system* to protect itself from its own failure. The state apparatus was the legal and political structure that enabled it to do so.

Without the state the money system is nothing. Alternatives to money and the money system, therefore, are not just technical issues but *political* ones as well.

'Monetary phenomena are *always* and *everywhere* polit-ical.'[201] Genuine political power – that is, control over the state apparatus at a national and international level – is what facilitates the capitalist shaping of our money system to suit the ends of capitalist accumulation (capital begets capital).

If we want to challenge the current use of the money system and build a more progressive society, we need to factor in ways to shape the state apparatus to suit that end. The purpose is to build a money system, an econ-omy and a society that 'puts life and everything neces-sary to produce and maintain life on this planet at the centre of economic and political activity and not the nev-er-ending accumulation of dead money'.[202] This cannot be done in the absence of a political strategy and organ-isation, and possible ways to achieve these ends will be the topic of our final chapter, which looks at alternatives.

A Progressive Response

INTRODUCTION

When we talk of alternatives to money, what is it we are actually putting forward? Is it alternatives to currency, the standard unit of account which also acts as a store of value and medium of exchange? Are we talking about alternatives to the things we use as money, that is, notes, coins and bank balance sheets? Would either or both of these changes be enough to build a more progressive society?

From the very start of this book the argument has been made that money is not an object but a social technology and a powerful one at that. The purpose to which that technology is put is not dictated by the money thing itself – notes, coins or balance sheets – but by the society in which it operates. The rules of football do not come from the football, but from the organisations that control football. Rules matter, and the rules of money today are the rules of capitalism.

The topic here is money, of course, not capitalism, but let us not pretend that the two can be separated. Capitalism is a 'way of arranging human society, of organizing the social relations of production, exchange, consumption, and distribution'[203] and the money system is absolutely critical to that process; it would be impossible for capitalism to work the way it does were it not for the money system and the way it is structured today. The purpose of capitalism, its *raison d'être*, is capital accumulation – capital begets capital – and it achieves this through its use of four fundamental elements of the capitalist economy:

1. the monetary system and bank-credit money

2. market exchange

3. private enterprise production of commodities and services

4. the state (to ensure the dominance of capital and subordination of labour).[204]

This brings us back to obstacles. The reason capitalism will not concede any of the control it has over the money system should be clear at this point; without that control capitalism would find it difficult (maybe even impossible) to continue its quest for capital accumulation. The core issue then is not whether there is a working alternative to the things we use as money, but whether there is a working alternative to the logic and purpose to which money is put today. Can we change the money system *within capitalism* or do we need to get rid of capitalism altogether? Whatever option is taken, how best can it be achieved? What are the tools we need, and how do we get our hands on them?

This chapter will begin by critically analysing some influential proposals on how to address the logic of the money system by putting in place more progressive and equitable laws and structures. It will then look at important and often neglected frameworks for thinking about what reform might involve and the principles underpinning it, before finishing with a discussion of the importance of collective organisation towards progressive change in Ireland. In one respect, what is being put forward is quite modest. This is not to dismiss a radical and revolutionary agenda but simply makes the point that revolution has its own dynamic; it is, by its very nature, a resetting of the rules of engagement. The issue is what can be done in the absence of such an event to move things forward, as acquiescence to the status quo is not an option.

It will also make the point that when it comes to reforming the monetary system, modest proposals are rarely achieved through modest means; the methods used to win your demands are not dictated by the nature of your demands, but by the scale of opposition to them. Capitalism is a formidable opponent, one that is not known for playing fair, even by the rules it sets. The goal of a progressive monetary and financial system will not be secured through blogs, retweets, or letters to *The Irish Times*. Capitalism, and the money system it controls, will not be brow-beaten into submission. There is not a tut-tut that has been invented that will compel capitalism to change its ways. 'Much of the way we organise the economic aspects of modern life is ethically and politically indefensible, and ecologically suicidal,' wrote the academic and activist Geoff Mann, but 'merely pointing that out, and then waiting for everyone to agree, is a mostly futile exercise'.[205]

Societal change of any kind requires organisation. It requires planning, ideas, objectives and strategy. It also requires an ongoing *reflection*. How do we improve on the tactics that work and can we discard the ones that don't? Do we need to modify our ideas as we begin to see their blind spots? A progressive vision comes alive through action, the experience of which feeds back into the vision, which is again tested through action. We have ideas, we put them into practice, we see what works and what doesn't, and we adapt and move on, a process known as praxis. It is key to achieving real change.

In terms of ideas, we need to ask ourselves whether the inequalities caused by our monetary and financial systems are moral or structural failings. This is not an academic exercise; the conclusions reached have implications for how we organise for progressive change. By way of example, let us return to the Irish bank crisis and the economic interests that revealed themselves through it.

In 2009 the journalist Fintan O'Toole wrote that 'stupidity and corruption' led to the Irish bank crisis.[206] 'The role of sheer idiocy,' he said, 'should not be understated.'[207] His journalist colleague Arthur Beesley said that the directors of Irish Life and Permanent, one of the banks with the biggest losses, inhabited an 'ethical cocoon in which the sense of right and wrong [was] at odds with standards in the outside world'.[208] The economist Brian Lucey talked of the immorality and unfairness of NAMA, which was one of the conduits for the bank bailout.[209] Outside of Ireland the former chancellor and leader of the British Labour Party, Gordon Brown, said that the lack of a 'consistently high code of standards' among bankers was partly to blame for the global crisis, and so a strong sense of morality needed to return to economic policy and planning.[210]

Moral arguments resonate. Very few of us need or require a systemic analysis to get through our everyday lives. At a micro level personal judgement comes into play and it is understandable that we would take that template and apply it to economics, politics and the state. When we get to a systemic level, however, a different dynamic kicks in. The outcome of the interaction between different elements of a system cannot be reduced to any one element of that system. The interaction between the different parts produces an energy that cannot be produced alone.

In snooker, the cue ball hits the red ball and the red ball moves. A hits B leading to C. It is simple cause and effect. A car engine is comprised of cylinders, pistons, spark plugs, valves, a crankshaft and fuel. All these different elements have to interact with each other at the same time in order to produce motion. It is the *interaction* between the significant elements that makes the engine work. We may think of the fuel as the main factor, but a car will not move in the absence of a spark plug or a piston or a crankshaft. It is a dynamic system. The whole is more than the sum of the parts. When we analyse a financial and economic system we are looking at something that is connected in ways that cannot be captured by cause and effect. Unfortunately, that was not the way mainstream economics saw it.

On 23 October 2008 the former head of the Federal Reserve, Alan Greenspan, gave evidence to the US House Committee on Oversight and Government Reform as part of its hearings into the financial crisis.[211] He was asked by the committee chairman, Henry Waxman, if he felt that his free-market ideology had pushed him to make decisions that he wished he had not made. 'Yes,' said Greenspan, 'I found a flaw, I don't know how significant or permanent it is, but I have been very distressed by that fact.' 'In other words,' said Waxman to Greenspan, 'you found that your view of the world, your ideology, was not right, it was not working.' 'Precisely,' said Greenspan.

Willem Buiter, former Professor of European Political Economy at the London School of Economics, also commented on the failure of mainstream economic ideology to predict and cope with the crisis. Buiter was a founder member of the Bank of England Monetary Policy Committee which had, as one would expect, 'quite a strong representation of academic economists and other professional economists with serious technical training and backgrounds'.[212] 'This turned out to be a severe handicap', once the financial crisis hit, said Buiter, as the conceptual frameworks necessary to address it were not on the table. 'Indeed,' said Buiter, 'the typical graduate macroeconomics and monetary economics training received at Anglo-American universities during the past 30 years or so, may have set back by decades serious investigations of aggregate economic behaviour and economic policy-relevant understanding.' 'It was,' he said, 'a privately and socially costly waste of time and other resources.'

Modern mainstream macroeconomics has produced an army of specialists ever hearing but never understanding; ever seeing but never perceiving. It has created a model of the world with no people in it, or certainly not the people that you and I know. It has as much a relationship with actually existing humanity as the Marvel comic book universe, although at least Marvel acknowledges the existence of women. Macroeconomics might as well be talking about Thor and Wolverine when it talks of rational expectations man, a mythical beast – all-knowing, all-seeing and endowed with perfect knowledge at all times – who deserves his own section in Jorge Luis Borges' *The Book of Imaginary Beings*, between the Rain Bird and the Remora.

The fundamental concept the experts ignored was that of economics as a social connection; instead, they insisted that all human activity could be explained simply as market and monetary transactions. However, it is 'interactions and relationships *between* people', wrote the activist and trade unionist Jim Stanford, 'that make the economy go around'.[213] Markets are artificial, as are institutions, as is money. The fact that they are all human creations and the product of human decisions means that the social effects of those decisions are also the result of human activity.[214] There is no invisible hand. Anything made by people can be changed by people. Furthermore, the structural and systemic inequalities that arise as a result of markets and institutions demand a structural and systemic response.

In terms of Ireland, I will argue that a commonwealth of progressive civil society and trade union organisations is needed in order to effect structural, progressive change. It will also act to protect any progressive gains made when Irish capitalism (with the help of state institutions) counter-attacks. But first, we will start with the types of changes that could be made to the present system, before moving on to how to implement them.

IDEAS

The desire to express the wilful chaos of a capitalist-controlled monetary system as personal moral failure is a quixotic pursuit, chasing windmills, not dragons. 'Debates over economic issues are not technical debates where expertise alone settles the day,' wrote Stanford, 'they are deeply political debates.'[215] Within these debates, economic ideology is the weapon of choice. It is not the purpose of mainstream macroeconomics to explain the world; its purpose is to justify a political project that shapes the world to suit powerful economic interests – in our world, the goal of capital accumulation. 'Economics provides an ideological justification for atavistic methods of providing for our economic and social needs,' wrote the American economist Michael Perelman. 'It leads to economic practices that create great harm to both people and the environment.'[216]

The truth is that economic inequality – however immoral it may be – is still a political process. We can pass a moral judgement on it, but it exists because of the way our society is structured. 'The history of the distribution of wealth has always been deeply political, and it cannot be reduced to purely economic mechanisms,' wrote the French economist Thomas Piketty, in his unexpected bestseller, *Capital in the Twenty-First Century*.[217] He said that 'the history of inequality is shaped by the way economic, social, and political actors view what is just and what is not, as well as by the relative power of those actors and the collective choices that result'.[218] 'Furthermore,' he wrote, 'there is no natural, spontaneous process to prevent destabilizing, inegalitarian forces from prevailing permanently.'[219] In other words, whatever damage capitalism does to itself will not be enough to make it change its ways. The wringing of hands and the appeal to the better angels of its nature will achieve very little. Morality serves no existential threat to inequality.

For that reason, Piketty rejected such an approach. He argued that inequality of a socially destructive nature occurs when the rate of return on capital (that is, money used as investment) is greater than the rate of growth for the economy. It is the core of his book and is expressed in the following equation:

$$R > G$$

The symbol R stands for the average rate of return on capital including profits, interest, fees, rents, dividends and other such income. The symbol G stands for the annual increase in national income or output. When the return on capital is greater than the actual growth generated through productivity, inequality increases.

Piketty brings us right back to the money system and the way it operates under capitalism. The search for yield on capital investment takes place regardless of the social and economic implications of that investment. The ideology of capitalism says that the market will compensate, but of course it does not. Left unchecked, the search for yield destabilises society and, for Piketty, the way to address this is through taxation.

'The ideal policy for avoiding an endless inegalitarian spiral and regaining control over the dynamics of accumulation,' wrote Piketty, 'would be a progressive tax on capital.'[220] Such a tax would serve two objectives: it would 'promote the general interest over private interests while preserving economic openness and the forces of competition'.[221] This would require legislation, which requires political organisation. In other words, Piketty sees politics as the conduit for change and social justice. 'Such questions will never be answered by abstract principles or mathematical formulas,' he wrote. 'The only way to answer them is through democratic deliberation and political confrontation.'[222]

Piketty, therefore, gives us a way to confront the logic of a capitalist money system – taxation – and a way to achieve this end – politics. He is adamant that this is not a technical issue to be sorted out by experts, but a *political* one that requires democratic input and debate. Furthermore, Piketty sees taxation not solely in terms of raising revenue, but also as a mechanism for ameliorating the socially destructive investment strategies of financial investors. His call for a progressive taxation system is one that seeks to bring stability to the financial system and a new social state for the twenty-first century. This would be based around 'a logic of rights and a principle of equal access to a certain number of goods deemed to be fundamental'.[223] He sees it as 'financing public services and replacement incomes that are more or less equal for everyone, especially in the areas of health, education and pensions'.[224]

The academic and former World Bank economist Joseph Stiglitz also sees alternatives in a social state framework but places a greater emphasis on the organisational networks needed to achieve progressive change. In *Rewriting the Rules of the American Economy: An Agenda for Growth and Shared Prosperity*, Stiglitz said that his approach is 'based on two simple economic observations: rules matter and power matters'.[225] Rules include regulations and legal frameworks, but they also include 'institutions that perpetuate discrimination, including structural discrimination – an entire system of rules, regulations, expenditure, policies, and normative practices that exclude populations from the economy and economic opportunity'.[226] Stiglitz said that 'unequal socio-economic outcomes for women and people of colour are rooted in this kind of structural discrimination, in addition to other forms of bias'.[227] The challenge for progressives is to rewrite the rules so that they work for everyone.

Stiglitz wants to see an end to the 'distortions that pervade our financial sector, our corporate rules, our macroeconomic, monetary, tax, expenditure and competition policies, our labor relations and our political structures'.[228] He argues for better regulation of the financial sector; more competitive markets; a rebalanced tax system with a move away from corporate welfare and towards increased rates on capital gains and dividends; full employment as the main goal of monetary policy; strengthening the rights of workers; increasing the national minimum wage and empowering organised labour.

It is quite the shopping list, and appears radical, but again the objective is to ameliorate the excesses of capitalism, not to transform them. Stiglitz is making an argument for change, but the purpose is to put stabilisers on capitalism; the objective of self-expansion – of capital begets capital – will remain in place.

However, the plan is at least progressive and one that views the distribution of socially produced wealth from an equality perspective. Stiglitz wants to keep the two core elements of capitalism in place – the monetisation of social value and human labour, with the monetised output subject to private property rights – but he also wants its excesses reined in through the social distributive conduits of wages and taxation. Workers gain more of the monetised output through higher wages, while the state uses the greater taxation of capital to distribute socially produced wealth through investment in social services and physical infrastructure. 'Concentrated wealth can hurt economic performance,' wrote Stiglitz, but 'under the right rules, shared prosperity and strong economic performance reinforce each other. There is no trade-off.'[229] In order for this to happen, 'we must rewrite the rules of the economy with a focus on restoring a balance of power between the competing interests that make up the modern economy'.[230]

Both Piketty and Stiglitz highlight the need for a policy framework with a socially distributive agenda. They recognise that in order for this to happen, the state needs to play a coercive role to get capitalism to 'play fair' through rules, regulations and taxation. Both acknowledge that the unequal distribution of socially produced wealth is ultimately an issue of social and economic power. Both, however, refrain from discussing just how capitalism is to be challenged and coerced into making the concessions needed in order to produce a socially progressive and more stable society.

Piketty and Stiglitz see change as essentially an intellectual exercise of persuasion, albeit one where Stiglitz at least acknowledges the importance of trade union organisation. Although neither depends on an overtly moral framework for the progressive redistribution of socially produced wealth, they fall back on such a framework when it comes to challenging the embedded power of capitalism. This is where progressive social democracy starts to trail off. Social democrats will challenge ideas, but to directly challenge power takes a different type of activism.

The alternatives as represented by Piketty and Stiglitz are driven by a desire for the redistribution of socially produced wealth via wages and state services. This is also the core element of the post-war social democratic compromise between capitalism and labour. But this did not come about through a reasoned discussion with capitalism. It came about through class conflict. If progressives want to return to social democracy, they will still need to return to the type of societal conflict that brought capitalism to the negotiating table in the first place. There is no getting around this fact. In the words of Frederick Douglass, 'Those who profess to favor freedom and yet deprecate agitation are men who want crops without plowing up the ground; they want rain without thunder and lightning.'[231]

This brings us back once again to class struggle. The title of Piketty's book is a gauntlet thrown down to the earlier, more famous work by Marx first published in 1868. In that publication, simply called *Capital*, one key point of departure in analysis comes when Marx discusses the respective rights of capitalism and labour in terms of the working day:

The capitalist maintains his rights as a purchaser [of human labour] when he tries to make the working day as long as possible, and, where possible, to make two working days out of one. On the other hand, the peculiar nature of the commodity sold implies a limit to its consumption by the purchaser, and the worker maintains his right as a seller when he wishes to reduce the working day to a particular normal length. There is here therefore an antinomy of right against right, both equally bearing the seal of the law of exchange. Between equal rights, force decides.[232]

Marx does not frame his argument in terms of right versus wrong, but right versus right. 'Between equal rights, force decides.' Time and again, history shows us that it is not possible to sidestep the economic power relations of capitalism and the class antagonisms they produce; the agenda for such antagonisms is dictated by the prime objective of capitalism itself – capital begets capital – one for which capitalism requires control over the money system. The breakdown of the Bretton Woods Agreement saw finance capitalism shake off the constraints that John Maynard Keynes and Harry Dexter White tried to place upon it and re-emerge as a significant destabilising social force.

In 1989 the Marxist geographer David Harvey noted that 'something significant has changed in the way capitalism has been working since about 1970'.[233] He saw it as a process marked by 'the complete reorganization of the global financial system and the emergence of greatly enhanced powers of financial co-ordination'.[234] In his 2011 publication *The Rise and Fall of the Welfare State*, Asbjørn Wahl wrote that the origin of the welfare state came about through a shift in class power and that those power relations changed in the 1980s as a result of the neoliberal offensive. Since then 'strong capital interests and neoliberals have been fighting to undermine the most important institutions that maintain the welfare state', which he sees as 'the trade unions and democracy'.[235] We are witnessing at present social revenge, he added, 'where the economic and political elite in society have gone on the offensive in order to reconquer privileges they lost through the democratization, regulation and redistribution of the welfare state'.[236]

Wahl makes the argument that the ideology of social partnership, which underpins the welfare state, was a child of class compromise. It was the result of a very specific historical development which saw the balance of economic power shift towards labour. Capitalism in western democracies was compelled to address workers' demands in the face of the reality of the Soviet Union. Social partnership was as much a child of the Cold War as anything else. The relative social peace saw a depoliticising of trade unions. It changed the character of social democracy from a class movement to one based on mediation between classes. The current breakdown of the class compromise, which underpinned social democracy, has occurred at a time when the trade union movement, the traditional bulwark against capitalism, is at its weakest in decades. As a result, capitalism has recaptured lost ground.

Wahl makes the point that while we need alternatives to the ideas and arguments of the neoliberal turn we also need to consider agency, that is, we need to consider who is going to engage in the struggle and what social forces and alliances are needed to bring about progressive social change. He acknowledges that while trade unions have a weakened credibility at the moment, nonetheless the trade union movement has the *potential* to push the type of policies envisioned by writers such as Piketty and Stiglitz. Wahl argues that a commonwealth of progressive forces – trade union, community and political – is needed to tackle the logic of capitalism and improve ordinary people's lives once again.

In his 2012 publication *In Place of Austerity*, Dexter Whitfield summarised the present financial crisis as 'a failure of neoliberalism that prioritised deregulation, marketisation, competition, debt-driven consumerism, privatisation, and the erosion of democratic accountability and transparency'.[237] He explored not only the world of alternatives to capitalism but also tactics and strategies that oppose and weaken the grip that capital investment – in particular, speculative investment in financial products – has on our lives, our communities, our workplaces and our futures. He argued that we should not assume that anti-capitalist tactics by themselves constitute an anti-capitalist plan of action. 'Examples of successful campaigns elsewhere are important to illustrate what can be achieved and to give confidence,' he wrote, 'but they are not a substitute for strategy.'[238] This flaw is evident in what Piketty and Stiglitz present as solutions.

They give us *examples as strategy*, not *examples as part of an overall strategy*, and certainly not one which is willing to confront power directly. Their general frameworks are a poor substitute – an almost technocratic response – to what more and more people see as the most pressing need of our day: the need for a vibrant and sustainable alternative to capitalism and its control of the money system.

Whitfield echoes the arguments of Wahl and highlights the work of trade unions and community organisations across Europe in opposing the public spending cuts and increased charges for services, as well as outsourcing, job losses and wage reductions. However, he also makes the point that while resistance is crucial, it needs to be directed through an understanding of the prime directive of capitalism – capital begets capital. He points out that the policies of marketisation and privatisation 'are designed to create markets that lead to the transfer of government functions and service provision to the private sector'; that they are mechanisms for private capital 'to gain more power and control in the economy ... of transferring risk, cost and responsibility to individuals as a means of reducing the scope of the welfare state'; and that 'these policies are a means by which capital can radically reduce the role of the state, yet safeguard corporate welfare, which consists of tax breaks, subsidies, contracts and regulatory concessions'.[239] None of this has happened by accident. Finance capital needed to develop corporate welfare in the 1970s and 1980s as profit-seeking strategies within production began to stagnate. This reconstitution of profit-seeking activity within capitalism has led to profound realignments at a social, cultural, economic and political level. It is possible to see these dynamics in the rise of neo-liberalism. It is important to remind ourselves that the dominance of capital over labour in advanced capitalist countries, the whittling away of the post-world war compromise and New Deal policies, can mask somewhat the changes that have occurred *within* the capitalist class.

The realignment in economic power towards finance capital (in the wake of the breakdown of the Bretton Woods Agreement) has been achieved not only in the realm of the workplace but also in relation to monetary policy, in particular the emphasis on ultra-low inflation regardless of the social cost. The attack on trade union membership across the private and public sectors has been a boon to the employer and financier. At the same time the concurrent shift in economic power *within* the capitalist class – from producer-employer to rentier-financier – has been facilitated by the decline of the power of labour.

The 'war on inflation' is a proxy for the war on workers' rights and the social wage. 'It is no coincidence that the share of labour in GDP peaks in the 1970s for both the US and the UK,' wrote Ian Harnett and David Bowers in the *Financial Times* in 2013.[240] This was due in no small measure to the power of trade unions in securing the redistribution of socially generated wealth through wages and social services. The focus on lowering inflation from 1979 onwards was delivered 'at a cost of a declining share of labour in national income'; in other words, 'the fight against inflation amounted to a campaign to squeeze labour incomes.'[241]

This was part of a plan. In 1968, the Chicago School economist Harry Gordon Johnson argued in a paper on monetary economics that 'the avoidance of inflation [on the one hand] and the maintenance of full employment [on the other] can be most usefully regarded as conflicting class interests of the bourgeoisie and the proletariat, respectively' and that this conflict is resolvable 'only by the test of relative political power in the society and its resolution involving no reference to an overriding concept of the social welfare'.[242] In order to weaken the power of the labour movement to set wages, it needed to be challenged in the realm of state policy and social supports, and this had to be done in order to strengthen the profit-seeking strategies of capitalism. From Chile to Reagan, from Thatcher to the ECB, the war on inflation amounted to a war on labour and social cohesion. Harnett and Bowers' article highlights the relative weakness of the labour movement today. At the same time, however, it also recognises, albeit indirectly, that a strong labour movement has the capacity to address the power of capitalism, not only in the workplace but in the world of monetary and social policy as well.

In order for capitalism to thrive, the welfare of the workforce must be dismissed, and in order for capitalism to carry this out, it needs political power and the necessary determination to win at all costs. The history of Latin America in the 1970s, the US and UK in the 1980s, Russia and Asia in the 1990s, and Eurozone states in the 2010s paints a picture of just how ruthless capitalism is when it comes to class conflict. In an interview with *The New York Times* in November 2006, the billionaire Warren Buffett said that he thought it wrong that his cleaner ended up paying more tax as a percentage of her wage than he did. When the interviewer said that such comments were usually seen as talk of class warfare Buffett replied 'There's class warfare, all right, but it's my class, the rich class, that's making war, and we're winning.'[243] Capitalism operates through markets, the money system, and the state in order to achieve its objective of monetised self-expansion. It does not always get its own way and one of the more successful counter-capitalist forces, traditionally, has been organised labour.

'Even though the trade unions have been considerably weakened and driven back onto the defensive,' wrote Wahl, 'they are nevertheless the most important social force that can mobilize resistance' against austerity and the public costs of the financial bailouts.[244] This is not to say that the labour movement is the sole key point to transforming capitalism, only that it needs to be part of any overall strategy. At the very least the labour movement deserves our attention; it certainly has the attention of capitalism, which is constantly finding ways to limit the power of trade unions, and that should tell us something.

Political organisation is also an essential part of any strategy to counter the power of capitalism. As long as a state's laws are framed by parliament, then progressives not only need to have a voice there, but must also have a hand in steering the focus and direction of legislation. It is within this momentum – the political momentum – where the compromises and false starts are at their most acute. Nonetheless, it is crucial. The drive towards social transformation is political, as well as cultural and educational.

Political organisation and party structures are sometimes portrayed as a side show to the struggle for equality. It is as if the changes needed to transform society and the economy will be achieved by lobbying those already in power, coupled with good intentions. Again, it is possible to see why some may wish to avoid an overtly political dimension to this thesis. There is an overwhelming cynicism these days with all things political, and save for brief moments of genuine opportunity, the world of politics is one where radicals have to compromise the most, and for seemingly little gain. Yet, capitalism has not conceded the political to other forces. Indeed, it retains a tight grip on political power for the very reason that when used as part of a wider strategy, politics can bring transformative change. It is too important to be left out of the equation.

According to Whitfield, 'building alliances and coalitions between trade union, community and civil society organisations and taking action is essential to broaden and strengthen support'.[245] This is a call for a merging of campaigns and interests; it is not simply about platform-sharing or shared logos in a leaflet. Whitfield is drawing upon ideas emanating from Latin and North

America, in particular those associated with social movement unionism. In the words of the American academic and activist Dan Clawson, 'Rather than a united front of movements that remain separate and operate as partners, we need to abolish the distinctions between these movements.'[246] The labour movement, adds Clawson, 'must do more than build alliances; it must fuse with these movements such that it is no longer clear what is a labor issue and what is a women's issue or an immigrant issue'.

The logic of capitalism has a structural expression; therefore, it demands a structural response. It is not enough to socialise the output; the social and political mechanisms that create that output need to change as well. Nowhere is this seen more clearly than in the realm of social reproduction and what it can tell us in terms of how capitalism operates.

Capitalism exploits more work and production relations than just wage labor relations ...
Maria Mies and Veronika Bennholdt-Thomsen, 1999 [247]

In the summer of 1972, while neoliberal economics was working its way into government policy formation, a group of feminist activists from England, France, Italy and the US met in Padova, Italy and launched a new campaign based around wages for housework. 'Class struggle and feminism for us are one and the same thing,' they said in a statement to the journal *Off Our Backs*: 'We reject both class struggle as subordinate to feminism and feminism as subordinate to class struggle.' The group identified itself as Marxist-feminist and put forward a definition of class which incorporated the 'exploitation of the labour of women in the home and the cause of their more intense exploitation out of it'. The group said that 'such an analysis of class presupposes a new area of struggle',[248] the subversion not only of the factory and office but of the community. It saw two equal and interdependent struggles in the two areas of production – the home and the factory – and as such it was wrong to assume that the women's struggle was somehow secondary to that of class. 'This assumption of the auxiliary nature of women's struggle,' they said, 'flows directly from *the misconception that women's labour in the home is auxiliary to the reproduction and development of capital* [my emphasis], a misconception which has so long hindered us all.'

This idea was expanded upon in a pamphlet co-written by Mariarosa Dalla Costa and Selma James published the same year entitled *The Power of Women and the Subversion of the Community*. 'The community therefore is not an area of freedom and leisure auxiliary to the factory, where by chance there happen to be women who are degraded as the personal servants of men,' they said.[249] 'The community is the other half of capitalist organisation, the other area of hidden capitalist exploitation, *the other, hidden, source of surplus labour* [original emphasis].'[250] It was a continuation of a similar analysis put forward by the Canadian feminist activist Peggy Morton, in her seminal 1970 article 'Women's

Work is Never Done'. Morton saw that in order to fully understand capitalism it was necessary to 'see the family as a unit whose function is the maintenance of the reproduction of labour power', and that 'this conception of the family allows us to look at women's public (work in the labour force) and private (work in the family) roles in an integrated way'.[251]

Mainstream Marxist thought assumed a division of work into productive and unproductive sectors, with 'factory' productive and 'household' unproductive. This was a fundamental misconception, a blind spot to the manner in which capitalism operates. The family is a social factory; it is central to capitalism's imperative of self-expansion through monetisation. The household is the space where human labour is produced, maintained and reproduced, the cost of which is borne by the household. Capitalism does not willingly pay for the reproduction of the labour it exploits. Social democracy forced it to contribute to this reproduction through legislation and general taxation, but from the 1970s onwards these very supports have been under profound attack by capitalism, in particular finance capital. The slashing of corporation and capital taxes is the slashing of capital's contribution to the social reproduction of human labour, pushing the burden back onto the shoulders of ordinary people and women in particular. Austerity is a continuation of this process. It is class war writ large, with gendered consequences.

The attack on social services brings the capitalist accumulation imperative into the realm of social reproduction. Work in this sphere is usually carried out by women in addition to their paid wage labour. When progressives discuss growth, they tend to do so through assumptions that see human activity as a tripartite of profit-seeking work, consumption and leisure. A proposal by the American sociologist Erik Olin Wright, for example, to 'reengineer the economy in the rich regions of the world in such a way that increases in leisure would be given priority over increases in consumption',[252] is one that still remains chained to the conceptual framework of capitalist-led analysis. There is more to growth than simply positing the *absence* of profit-seeking growth.

In 2011 the London-based group Feminist Fightback argued that 'over the past thirty years, despite their being essential to human life, neoliberal restructuring across the world has privatised, eroded and demolished our shared resources, and ushered in a crisis of social re-production'.[253] The drive to dismantle the welfare state in its various guises has the effect of placing more pressure on women in their 'double shift' to compensate for the withdrawal of the state from this arena of social necessity. Feminist Fightback focus in on this aspect of austerity 'not because we think this is the only feminist issue, or is only an issue for feminists, but because we see it as a productive way into thinking about how to build a movement that can mount a much broader challenge to the austerity drive'.[254]

The need for capitalism to enclose social reproduction for profit-seeking purposes makes the issue one that contains the potential for a genuine counter-attack against it. In the world of Feminist Fightback,

> An alliance between working mothers and childcare workers has radical potential. It would require – and therefore constitute – a significant shift in mentalities, thereby pushing against one of the key divisions from which capitalism has benefited. Bridging the distinction between waged/unwaged, productive/reproductive workers rejects the artificial distinctions between the two, while also confronting the very real issues which produce the divisions. This would not be an alliance to defend the current system, but to call for its transformation; for something better. Such alliances would also make visible the labour and economic impact of care work, confronting the logic at the heart of the government's representation of public services as a luxury extra.[255]

The counter-capitalist strategies put forward by the likes of Dalla Costa, James, Whitfield, and Feminist Fightback are ones that are fully cognisant of the fact that capitalism is an unequal and highly destructive power relation, and that today finance capital is the dominant strand of capitalism within the so-called 'advanced' economies of the US and Europe. In the case of Feminist Fightback, it brings an insight into the patriarchal nature of capitalism and the discipline of economics, which is generally used to decipher its code.

Cooperation among movements for societal change is nothing new, but the purpose of that cooperation, and its power, appears to have been forgotten. The way finance capital seeks profit and maintains power has an effect on the shape of our resistance to it. The ideas of social movement unionism and feminist economics serve to shine a light on ways of thinking and organisation that will complement the actions of those who wish to transform capitalism.

The political state is a contested space between capitalism and democratic ideals. There is a conflict between capitalist accumulation and social stability. We can see this in the ongoing 'crisis' of social reproduction. However, this crisis also gives us an opportunity for counter-capitalist organisation and resistance. There is a need for progressive trade unions, political and civil society groupings to come together and work towards the common goal of challenging the social instability that comes from the relentless capitalist 'hunt' for yield.

Before returning to Ireland, we should pause and reflect for a moment. Political organisation, trade unionism, Marxist feminism – how are these alternatives to the money system? What about cryptocurrencies, or local exchange trading systems such as timebanks or local currencies with printed notes?[256] To echo the opening remarks of this chapter, money is not a thing but a social technology, one where the organisational and distributional logic of the society that uses that technology is the key issue, not the actual form the money takes.

Take, for example, bitcoin. Frequently described as an alternative currency, it is a child of the global financial crisis. It first appeared in 2009 and was summed up by the *Financial Times* in 2011 as 'what happens when you cross computer geeks with populist outrage at central banks'.[257] Bitcoins are created and distributed over a peer-to-peer network,[258] and the early developers set out 'to attract users by exploiting some people's disaffection with the government-controlled central banks that control conventional money'.[259]

The idea was to have bitcoin as an online medium of exchange and means of payment that was completely anonymous and outside of government oversight and control. 'Bitcoins have value simply by virtue of the fact that people are willing to accept them as payment for real goods and services,' said the *New Scientist* in 2011. That may have been true for a while, but then the logic of capitalism showed up, and bitcoin became a speculative asset in itself.

In 2011 one bitcoin was equivalent to €6; at the present time of writing (21 January 2018) it is €12,079. It is an asset wrapped up in a bubble. Bitcoin has 'value' today not because people want to use it to exchange for goods and services but because they are willing to speculate on its continued price growth. It is a Ponzi scheme, a classic capitalist venture. The computer geeks thought that the fault of the logic of the money system was in central banks and the money thing. They thought that if they made virtual money with its own network, that somehow the societal logic that underpins our society

– capital accumulation *via* things of value, a logic that proved so devastating in 2008 – could be sidelined and dismissed through the wonders of technology. But it can't. If you want to make a more equitable and democratic money system, you have to tackle the logic of capitalism, and that takes organisation and a plan. There is no virtual remedy for reality.

The only sphere of conflict that truly threatens the logic of capitalism is class conflict. However, we need to recognise that if we got rid of capitalism tomorrow through class conflict alone we would still have a lot of social and cultural inequalities to deal with and no real template for doing so, because a general strike does not shatter prejudice. It is important to show the true essence of capitalism. It lurks within the money system, which is portrayed by mainstream economics as a neutral space. This fallacy is reinforced by the political system and by state institutions. The class nature of the capitalist money system is often overlooked, as is the fact that credit systems are inherent to human societies. Capitalism is an *invasion* of the money system; it is not its creator.

When we look at alternatives to the logic of capitalism we need a greater canvas than just the exploitation of waged labour. We should have more ambition than simply ending exploitation in the sphere of monetised work. This means recognising that while wage labour and economic class inequality cannot be seriously tackled without class organisation and agitation, at the same time the other inequalities that capitalism engenders will not be addressed by such a strategy unless we make them so. As Maria Mies said, capitalism is more than just the relation between wage labour and capital. Unpaid labour in the realm of social reproduction is as crucial as the factory floor to the monetisation of human labour and social value. We simply cannot tackle capitalism through the sphere of waged work alone; we also need to tackle the exploitation of gendered and mostly unwaged social reproduction, as capitalism draws its strength and energy from both.

Progress is a commonwealth of energy and ideas. In his 1986 publication *Stabilizing an Unstable Economy*, the economist Hyman Minsky wrote that 'because what happens in our economy is so largely determined by financial considerations, economic theory can be relevant only if finance is integrated into the structure of theory'.[260] The same can be said of social theory and progressive alternatives. We avoid capitalism's use of the money system at our peril, for it will not avoid us. In the case of Ireland, that logic is slowly suffocating our social supports. A commonwealth of resistance, as outlined by Wahl, Whitfield and Feminist Fightback, is desperately needed.

IRELAND

There is a lot more to class than accent or dialect. It is a power relation, the dynamics of which have shaped the contours of the Irish state since its establishment over ninety years ago in the courtyard of Dublin Castle. The economic interests of Ireland's moneyed class have had an inordinate influence on our laws and on the scope and direction of government policies. It has been able to do this because its objectives and operational procedures are deeply embedded within the institutions of the state itself. It is without doubt the greatest block to progressive change in Ireland.

Take housing, for example. It is no secret that today in 2018 we are in the midst of a housing crisis and the way to solve it is to build more houses. The problem is not the solution, which is refreshingly self-evident, but rather the question of whose economic interests should be served or sidelined by whatever plan is put in place. Should we protect the financial interests of speculators and hope that they do the right thing, or should we protect ordinary households because we know that speculators will only ever look after themselves?

The housing plans put forward by successive governments were designed in such a way as to ensure that the speculative price of a house will continue to rise. The government will try to help people 'afford' that price but it will not do anything to dampen, stall or reverse its upward ascent. It will say that property speculators need the right encouragements to build, and that the best incentive for them is a rising market. Meanwhile, accommodation is out of reach for ordinary households and this is compounded by official state policy.

The problem is that we are not just dealing with the relationship between property speculators and political parties; we are also talking about banks, land-hoarders, estate agents, insurance companies, the Department of Finance, the Central Bank, the Revenue Commissioners, tax lawyers, the Housing Agency, Real Estate Investment Trusts (Reits), the Department of the Taoiseach, and the Department of Housing and Local Government. The plans of all of these companies, agencies and institutions are framed by the logic of capital accumulation. They have a shared economic interest and common cultural and intellectual reference points, and these are not due to nor exclusively held by any one person or group. These economic class interests have an institutional form; they are supported and maintained by the state apparatus and by the way the state operates. They are deeply embedded in our legal and taxation systems, both of which prioritise the interests of speculators and financiers over the common good. They are imbedded throughout our banks as well as in the regulators and the policy units of our government departments.

There has been in Ireland a forty-year move to shut down social housing, and the class that has benefited from this will not allow any crisis for ordinary people to reverse the trend. In fact, the selling-off of our public housing stock, the almost complete privatisation of the rental sector, and the creation of the myth that home ownership 'is in our DNA' has been one of the great ideological successes of that class.[261] They are not going to give that up for anyone.

It is not just in housing that this class flexes its muscles; it is in workers' rights as well. On 28 September 2017 Regina Doherty, the Minister for Employment

Affairs and Social Protection, appeared before the Joint Oireachtas Committee for Social Protection and proceeded to defend proposed new laws that would further erode the livelihoods of ordinary working people. The minister said that she wanted to introduce measures to ban zero-hour contracts, but that she also wanted to insert a caveat to ensure that 'work of a casual nature' was exempt from the legislation. She was challenged on the idea of a law that would allow the continuation of the very thing it is supposed to ban, but Regina Doherty was not for turning. The law would stand as drafted, she said, before going on to criticise the committee for being so negative.

Trade unions and civil society groups can lobby government and hope to influence the outcome, but in general Irish state departments will bow to the logic of capital accumulation, with nothing but the weakest of concessions to fairness and social cohesion. This leads us to the situation we have now: a minister who says she will ban zero-hour contracts – except in cases where bosses want to use them – and will force workers to apply for a work contract under exploitative terms. This is coupled with a housing policy that is designed to benefit speculators and financiers over ordinary people. The pursuit of capital accumulation is only possible because of the capture of markets, the money system, and the state, by the logic of capitalism. There is simply no way to change or modify the money system alone to make it more equitable, nor is it possible without provoking a strong and stiff reaction from the moneyed interests that have a vested stake in the control of that system. Progressives need an organisational class strength to challenge it.

But it is not enough to look at capitalism simply in terms of economic class alone, for if we do so we are in danger of missing out on the gendered nature of how capitalism works. Given the debate that exists at the moment – that somehow feminism and identity issues 'distract' from the struggle against capitalism – let me state clearly: nothing could be further from the truth. It is simply impossible to confront capitalism and not confront the exploitation of women through gendered roles and economic position in society. This is not some kind of moral response on the part of progressives, that we should do it because it is 'the right thing to do'; the struggle against the economic exploitation of women through gendered roles is a struggle against capitalist accumulation itself. That is a fact. Any progressive movement worth its salt ignores that at its peril.

Irish progressives should embrace all of the elements discussed – in terms of politics, gender and organised labour – in a commonwealth of trade unions, civil society and political representation. We need to do this in order to shape our own future. The alternative to the current situation of seeing the interests of Ireland's moneyed classes made law is quite straightforward: we make the laws ourselves. And in order to do that, we need to organise.

Class power and class interests cannot be tackled at an individual level. The only thing that can take on

deeply embedded class interests is a counter-class organisation. In other words, if we want to take on those
who are organised at a class and state level then we
need to do the same; we also need to organise at a class
level with the aim of shaping the direction of the state
in a progressive way. But again, whereas the solution is
somewhat straightforward, the pathway to it is fraught
with tensions, contradictions and compromises.

Societies are never static. It is simply impossible for
them to be so for they have millions of moving parts.
Society is in a constant state of development; it is an
ongoing process. Institutions, however, are a different matter. Once a class interest takes an institutional
form it is very difficult to dislodge it. The issue that con-
fronts us today is not so much societal, but institutional change. We want the state to be reflective of where
we have already arrived in our thinking. The question
is how do we harness the change that is happening and
give it an institutional expression? How do we replace
the old conservatism and embedded financial interests
with the new in terms of social solidarity, and how do we
do it without making things worse? Without a workable
method of implementation any vision put forward of a
progressive and equal Ireland is merely an aspiration. It
is a set of words that serves no threat to power and its
institutions. In order to tackle Irish moneyed class interests and their control of the money system we therefore
need a commonwealth of civil society and trade unions
working in tandem with a progressive political sphere.

No plan survives contact with reality. The more intricate the design, the more likely it will fail. To coin an old phrase, 'Man plans and God laughs'.[262] The strategies that work are the ones that leave room for creativity and spontaneity. They have to do this, for the world has a way of throwing curve balls that knock you over when you least expect them. This means that a progressive movement cannot simply follow a plan as if life is some sort of predetermined pathway. A progressive movement needs: a set of objectives; an organisational structure to harness the societal energy that is out there for progressive change; a plan on how to achieve those objectives; and crucially, the ability to think and rethink the plan while it is in operation. The objectives stay the same; the flexibility is in the methods we adopt to get there. It's about education, campaigns, legislation and resources, all framed by class consciousness – that is, an awareness and understanding of how class works in Ireland, its economic and gendered necessities and the organisational solidarity needed to tackle it.

We need an organisational structure that is robust enough to make our objectives real, flexible enough to allow us to achieve them, and reflective enough of the particular and specific class antagonisms and gendered exploitations that are at play in this state to allow us to confront the class that opposes us. This is one thing we are going to have to work out for ourselves. We are going to have to teach ourselves to think about how Ireland works. We need to develop these skills, so we can adapt our strategies ourselves as circumstances arise.

The skill of thought and reflection is often labelled as education, but it has little if anything to do with school or experts. Activist education, done properly, does not teach you how Ireland works, it teaches you *to think* about how Ireland works and it does that for a very specific and practical reason: activists are on the ground and they need to be able to adapt strategies when the need arises. They need to be able to think clearly about how to achieve the same objectives, but by different means.

When we talk about education we are talking about a way of harnessing the experience and creativity of activists and placing that energy within a conceptual framework of economic class and gendered power relations and how they operate in Ireland today. Education used in this way simply gives direction and focus to what is already there. Education is not knowledge; it is understanding. It is not passive; it is active. Education is a tool that builds a deeper understanding of class as a power relation by using the knowledge and experience of activists on the ground. A movement that is able to think for itself – genuinely think for itself – is genuinely transformative.

It is entirely achievable.

Conclusion

The greatest trick that capitalism ever played was convincing the world that money was neutral. It was able to do this because money exists in an abstract and opaque space, with its own language and gatekeepers to knowledge. As citizens we are required to support the profit-seeking strategies of financial institutions that have significant control over money and credit, but we are not supposed to question those strategies, the logic that underpins them, nor the power relations that envelop that world. Money is just a thing, the economists say, one that is too complicated for ordinary and feeble minds.

The purpose of this book has been to show that, far from being neutral, money is an extremely powerful social technology, one that *demands* our attention. It 'consists of complex social practices that include power and class relationships, socially constructed meaning, and abstract representations of social value'.[263] There is nothing benign about the way societies construct themselves, an understanding of which is key to understanding money.

The rules that govern money today are those that serve the logic of capitalist accumulation. Indeed, the money system is absolutely crucial to the core objective of producing capital from capital and plays an active part in the creation and reproduction of social inequality. It makes possible the concentration of socially produced wealth in the hands of owners of capital, and because of this, capitalism will fight to the death to defend its control.

Ireland is fully integrated into the global capitalist money system. Although the country gained a form of political independence in 1922, it remained in a financial union with the UK for decades afterwards. The cost of this was staggering in terms of poverty and emigration due to the lack of indigenous investment and a fierce reluctance by the political establishment to force Irish banks to recycle savings in the state via credit formation. Since the 1980s Ireland has carved out for itself a niche role in global finance, facilitating tax evasion and loose regulation via its offshore financial centre, the IFSC. This is protected by the elites that profit from it, to the detriment of the rest of Irish society.

When it comes to alternatives to money, then, we should not fall into the bear trap that capitalism has set for us and pretend that it is a thing that can be changed, like a carpet that has faded with time. Any adaptation of money that leaves the logic of capitalist accumulation intact is no change at all, and capitalism will gleefully allow the experiment to run its course. The only way to truly tackle the inequalities facilitated by the money system is to tackle head-on the underlying logic, that is, capitalism itself. This means addressing the work and gender inequalities that capitalism exploits both in the workplace and in the sphere of social reproduction.

For us in Ireland today, that means a political strategy, one that involves civil society, organised labour and political representatives working in tandem with agreed objectives in terms of work, health, housing, childcare, education and taxation. A commonwealth of progressive forces is needed in order to realise those objectives and to defend them from capitalism when it counter-attacks. The direction that this collective action might take is something that can only be worked out through praxis – through action and reflection – and because of this its shape and form cannot be predicted with any certainty. It is a project that requires ongoing education, research, organisation and activism, if it is to have any chance of success. This will not be easy, but it can be done.

We should never see money in the way that capitalism wants us to see it. The objective here has been to shine a light on how money works, and for whom, so we can finally start using it to benefit society as a whole, and not just the alchemists of capitalist accumulation who need to be flung back into the medieval cage from which they sprung.

Notes and References

1. Letter from ECB [Jean-Claude Trichet] to Tánaiste on emergency liguidity assistance, 19 November 2010. *Evidence of Report of the Joint Committee of Inquiry into the Banking Crisis*. Dept. of Finance Core Booklet 21, p. 182. DOT00376-002. The purpose of emergency liguidity assistance (ELA) is to provide central bank money to financial institutions that are facing liquidity problems. It is used in cases where a financial institution is solvent but unable to adequately fund itself through normal market transactions.

2. The Troika were the European Commission, the ECB and IMF.

3. Nicholas Gregory Mankiw, *Macroeconomics*, 9th edn (New York: Worth Publishers, 2016), p. 82.

4. International Federation for Human Rights, *Downgrading Rights: The Cost of Austerity in Greece* (Athens: FIDH, 2014), p. 69.

5. Ibid.

6. Aldo Caliara, Sally-Anne Way, Natalie Raaber, Anne Schoenstein, Radhika Balakrishan and Nicholas Lusiani, *Bringing Human Rights to Bear in Times of Crisis* (New York: ESCR-Net, 2010), p. 11.

7. Not all of the interests that were 'bailed out' by the guarantee were financial. The state institutions that had failed to properly regulate the financial sector also needed the blanket guarantee to cover up their own mistakes. It was a desperate attempt on their part to buy more time to protect themselves.

8. Tim O'Brien, 'Bank Chief Calls for Brave Budget', *Irish Times*, 6 October 2008.

9. Simon Carswell, 'Foreign-owned Irish Banks Lobby to Be Included in State Guarantee', *Irish Times*, 1 October 2008. As soon as it became clear the guarantee was a disaster, Lenihan made the claim that Trichet told him to save the banks at all costs. This was flatly denied by Trichet when he spoke to members of the Bank Inquiry Committee on 30 April 2015. Trichet's exact words: 'I have not said that to Brian.' Trichet's evidence was more in line with Lenihan's contemporaneous account than with the post-bailout 'at all costs' justification for a horrendous decision. See 'Trichet, Jean-Claude', in *Report of the Joint Committee of Inquiry into the Banking Crisis, Volume 3: Evidence* (Dublin: Stationery Office, 2016), paragraph 1126.

10. Ben Hall, 'EU to Show United Front on Bank Bail-out Plan' *Financial Times*, 13 October 2008.

11. Morgan Kelly, 'Things Are Going to Get Much Worse', *Irish Times*, 24 October 2008.

12. For more on this see chapters 5 and 6 of C. McCabe, *Sins of the Father: The Decisions that Shaped the Irish Economy*, 2nd edn (Dublin: History Press Ireland, 2013), pp. 181–224.

13. William K. Tabb, *The Long Default: New York City and the Urban Fiscal Crisis* (New York: Monthly Review Press, 1982), p. 20.

14. Immanuel Wallerstein, *Historical Capitalism* (London: Verso, 1983), p. 14.

15. Ellen Meiksins Wood, *Democracy Against Capitalism: Renewing Historical Materialism* (London: Verso, 2016), p. 30.

16. Jim Stanford, *Economics for Everyone: A Short Guide to the Economics of Capitalism* (London: Pluto Press, 2008), p. 5.

17. Myles Horton and Paula Freire, *We Make the Road by Walking* (Philadelphia: Temple University Press, 1990), p. 102.

18. Geoffrey Ingham, *Capitalism* (Cambridge: Polity Press, 2008), p. 67.

19. Christine Desan, *Making Money: Coin, Currency, and the Coming of Capitalism* (Oxford: Oxford University Press, 2014), p. 1.

20. Catherine Eagleton and Jonathan Williams, *Money: A History*, 2nd edn (London: British Museum Press, 2011), p. 11.

21. Martha T. Roth, *Law Collections from Mesopotamia and Asia Minor*, 2nd edn (Atlanta: Scholars Press, 1997), p. 96.

22. William Stanley Jevons, *Money and the Medium of Exchange* (New York: D. Appleton & Co., 1875), p. 3.

23. Ibid.

24. Caroline Humphrey, 'Barter and Economic Disintegration', *Man*, vol. 20, no. 1 (March 1985), p. 48.

25. 'Economic historians have occasionally maintained that evolution in economic intercourse has proceeded from a natural or barter economy to a money economy and ultimately to a credit economy. This view was put forward, for example, in 1864 by Bruno Hildebrand of the German historical school of economics; it happens to be wrong.' C.P. Kindleberger, *A Financial History of Western Europe* (London: George Allen & Unwin, 1984), p. 21. Kindleberger was published thirty-three years ago and even then it was hardly a revolutionary text. The continued teaching of barter as the origin of money in Irish universities is, at this stage, on a par with creationism.

26. Steven J. Garfinkle, 'Shepherds, Merchants and Credit: Some Observations on Lending Practices in Ur III Mesopotamia', *Journal of the Economic and Social History of the Orient*, vol. 47, no. 1 (2004), p. 9.

27. Roth, *Law Collections*, p. 97. The interest in the example here worked out at 33 per cent on barley and 20 per cent on silver. It should be noted that interest rates were usually calculated on a per-loan basis.

28. Garfinkle, 'Shepherds, Merchants and Credit', p. 16.

29. Ibid., p. 24.

30. Ibid., p. 25.

31. David Graeber, *Debt: The First 5,000 Years* (Brooklyn: Melville House Publishing, 2011), p. 52.

32. Ibid.

33. Ibid., p. 130.

34. Ibid., p. 158.

35. Marilyn Gerriets, 'Money in Early Christian Ireland According to the Irish Laws', *Comparative Studies in Society and History*, vol. 27, no. 2 (1985), p. 329.

36. As an introduction for the general reader, see Graeber, *Debt*, chapters 2 to 7.

37. Peter Spufford, *Money and its Use in Medieval Europe* (Cambridge: Cambridge University Press, 1988), p. 9.

38. Ibid., pp. 14–16.

39. Ibid., p. 9.

40. Christine Desan, 'Coin Reconsidered: The Political Alchemy of Commodity Money', *Theoretical Inquiries in Law*, vol. 11, no. 1 (2010), p. 370.

41. Ibid.

42. A modern-day example of this is bitcoin, which is traded as an asset rather than used as a medium of exchange.

43. Fernand Braudel, *Civilisation and Capitalism 15th–18th Century, Volume 1: The Structures of Everyday Life* (London: Fontana Press, 1985), p. 462.

44. Yasha Beresiner and C.C. Narbeth, *The Story of Paper Money* (Bath: Pitman Press, 1973), p. 9.

45. Eagleton and Williams, *Money: A History*, p. 149.

46. Marco Polo, *The Travels of Marco Polo* (Edinburgh: Oliver & Boyd, 1845), pp. 137–8.

47. Richard Werner, *Princes of the Yen: Japan's Central Bankers and the Transformation of the Economy* (London: Routledge, 2003), p. 41.

48. Philip Jones, *The Italian City-State From Commune to Signoria* (Oxford: Clarendon Press, 1997), p. 198.

49. Ingham, *Capitalism*, p. 108.

50. Ibid.

51. Ibid.

52. Ibid., p. 72.

53. K.H.D. Haley, *The Dutch in the Seventeenth Century* (London: Thames & Hudson, 1972), p. 40.

54. Quoted in Braudel, *Civilization and Capitalism*, p. 235.

55. Ellen Meiksins Wood, *The Origin of Capitalism: A Longer View*, (London: Verso, 2002), p. 75.

56. Ellen Meiksins Wood, 'Capitalism's Gravediggers', *Jacobin*, 12 May 2014, https://www.jacobinmag.com/2014/12/capital-isms-gravediggers/ (accessed 20 December 2017).

57. Wood, *The Origin of Capitalism*, p. 3.

58. Wallerstein, *Historical Capitalism*, p. 18.

59. Ibid., p. 40.

60. Ibid., p. 19.

61. 'The persecution of witches (like the slave trade and the enclosures) was a central aspect of the accumulation and formulation of the modern proletariat, in Europe as well as in the "New World"'. Silvia Federici, *Caliban and the Witch* (Brooklyn: Autonomedia, 2004), p. 14.

62. Joseph Schumpeter, *History of Economic Analysis* (New York: Oxford University Press, 1986), p. 78, n. 1.

63. Geoffrey Ingham, *The Nature of Money* (Cambridge: Polity Press, 2004), p. 107.

64. Henry Maxwell, *Mr. Maxwell's Second Letter to Mr. Romley; Wherein the Objections against the Bank are Answered* (Dublin, 1721), p. 26.

65. Josiah Child, *A Discourse of the Nature, Use and Advantage of Trade* (London, 1694), p. 7.

66. 'For Josiah Child, "all riches and power, as well as private families, consists in comparison". An exchange that enriches both parts was not desirable, if it did not improve the power of

the nation relative to that of its exchange partner. Mercantilism presented a static conception of the economy, the world economic resources being supposedly fixed. The international economic relations are, therefore, characterised by an economic and military competition for foreign markets and resources.'
J. Fontanel , J.P. Hebert and I. Samson, 'The Birth of the Political Economy or the Economy in the Heart of Politics: Mercantilism', *Defence and Peace Economics*, vol. 19, no. 5 (2008), p. 333.

67. Carew Reynell, *The True English Interest* (London, 1674), p. 16.

68. Ibid., p. 17.

69. John Law, *Essay on a Land Bank* (London, 1705), p. 13.

70. Ingham, *Capitalism*, p. 125.

71. Stephen C.A. Pincus, 'A Revolution in Political Economy?' in Maximillian E. Novak (ed.), *The Age of Projects* (Toronto: University of Toronto Press, 2008), p. 126.

72. Ingham, *Capitalism*, p. 128.

73. Desan, *Coin Reconsidered*, p. 350.

74. Ingham, *Capitalism*, p. 128.

75. Karl Marx, *Capital: A Critique of Political Economy, vol. 1* (London: Penguin, 1990), p. 875.

76. Federici, *Caliban and the Witch*, p. 8.

77. Ibid.

78. Maria Mies and Veronika Bennholdt-Thomsen, *The Subsistence Perspective:* Beyond the Globalized Economy (London: Zed Books, 1999), p. 11.

79. United Nations Monetary and Financial Conference, *Bretton Woods, New Hampshire, July 1 to July 22, 1944, Final Act and Related Documents* (Washington: US Printing Office, 1944), p. 9.

80. Benn Steil, *The Battle of Bretton Woods: John Maynard Keynes, Harry Dexter White, and the Making of a New World Order* (Princeton: Princeton University Press, 2014), p. 10.

81. David M. Andrews, 'Bretton Woods: System and Order', in D. Andrews (ed), *Orderly Change: International Monetary Relations Since Bretton Woods* (Ithaca: Cornell University Press, 2008), p. 6.

82. *Joint Statement by Experts on the Establishment of an International Monetary Fund*, issued 21 April 1944. http://adlib. imf.org/digital_assets/wwwopac.ashx?command=getcontent&-server=webdocs&value=%5CBWC%5CBWC595-01.pdf (accessed 18 August 2012).

83. Eric Helleiner, 'From Bretton Woods to Global Finance: A World Turned Upside Down', in R. Stubbs and G.R.D. Underhill (eds), *Political Economy and the Changing Global Order* (London: Macmillan, 1994), p. 164.

84. Ibid.

85. Ibid.

86. Ibid.

87. Quoted in E. Helleiner, *States and the Reemergence of Global Finance: From Bretton Woods to the 1990s* (Ithaca: Cornell University Press, 1996), p. 25.

88. Michael Moffitt, *The World's Money: From Bretton Woods to the Brink of Insolvency* (New York: Simon & Schuster, 1983), p. 24.

89. Geoff Mann, *In the Long Run: Keynesianism, Political Economy and Revolution* (London: Verso, 2017), p. 274.

90. David Harvey, *A Brief History of Neoliberalism* (Oxford: Oxford University Press, 2005; 2007), pp. 10–11.

91. 'A scorpion asks a frog to carry it across a river. The frog hesitates, afraid of being stung, but the scorpion argues that if it did so, they would both drown. Considering this, the frog agrees, but midway across the river the scorpion does indeed sting the frog, dooming them both. When the frog asks the scorpion why, the scorpion replies that it was in its nature to do so.' https://en.wikipedia.org/wiki/The_Scorpion_and_the_Frog (accessed 3 January 2018).

92. Paul Einzig, 'Statics and Dynamics of the Euro-dollar Market', *The Economic Journal*, vol. 71, no. 283 (September 1961), p. 593.

93. 'A Billion Eurodollars', *The Economist*, 19 November 1960, p. 17.

94. Ibid.

95. 'Euro-Dollars Are Our Dollars', *The Economist*, 2 March 1963, p. 828.

96. Helleiner, *States*, p. 82.

97. Ibid., p. 84.

98. Ibid., p. 89.

99. Moffitt, *The World's Money*, p. 47.

100. Jocelyn Hambro, 'Hambros Bank: The Year of the Eurodollar', *The Economist*, 17 June 1967, p. 1281.

101. Einzig, 'Statics and Dynamics', p. 593.

102. Ibid.

103. John Hewson and Eisuke Sakakibara, *The Eurocurrency Markets and Their Implications: A New View of International Monetary Problems and Monetary Reform* (Lexington, Massachusetts: Lexington Books, 1975), p. 2.

104. John Eatwell and Lance Taylor, *Global Finance at Risk: The Case for International Regulation* (Cambridge: Polity Press, 2000), p. 3.

105. Ibid., p. 5.

106. Financial Crisis Inquiry Commission, *The Financial Crisis Inquiry Report* (New York: Public Affairs, 2011), p. xvii.

107. Gerald A. Epstein, 'Introduction: Financialization and the World Economy', in G.A. Epstein (ed), *Financialization and the World Economy* (Cheltenham: Edward Elgar, 2005), p. 3.

108. Greta R. Kripper, 'The Financialization of the American Economy', *Socio-Economic Review*, vol. 3, no. 2 (2005), p. 174.

109. Stanley Fish, 'Neoliberalism and Higher Education', *Opinionator: New York Times*, 8 March 2009, http://opinionator. blogs.nytimes.com/2009/03/08/neoliberalism-and-higher-education/ (accessed 15 April 2013).

110. John Quiggin, 'Neoliberalism Defined', http://johnquiggin. com/2008/09/27/neoliberalism-defined/ (accessed 15 April 2013).

111. Bjarke Skærlund Risager, 'Neoliberalism Is a Political Project: An Interview with David Harvey', *Jacobin*, 23 July 2016. https://www.jacobinmag.com/2016/07/david-harvey-neoliber-alism-

capitalism-labor-crisis-resistance (accessed 4 January 2018).

112. Ronen Palan, Richard Murphy and Christian Chavagneux, *Tax Havens: How Globalization Really Works* (Ithaca: Cornell University Press, 2010), p. 149.

113. The Paradise Papers was a huge leak of financial documents in 2017 that threw light on the world of offshore finance. https://www.icij.org/investigations/paradise-papers/ (accessed 4 January 2018).

114. Giovanni Arrighi, *The Long Twentieth Century: Money, Power and the Origins of Our Times*, 2nd edn (London: Verso, 2010), p. 8.

115. Chapter 3 will, however, briefly discuss bitcoin as emblematic of problems that I believe are associated with them.

116. United States Permanent Subcommittee on Investigations, *Repatriating Offshore Funds: 2004 Tax Windfall for Select Multinationals Majority Staff Report* (October 2011), p. 34. http:// www.hsgac.senate.gov/download/?id=a17c69df-38f1-479e-8612-a165e33b29a5 (accessed 10 November 2012).

117. EU Commission, *Commission Decision of 30.8.2016 on State Aid Sa.38373 (2014/C) (Ex 2014/Nn) (Ex 2014/Cp) Implemented by Ireland to Apple C(2016) 5605* (Brussels: EU Commission, 2016). http://ec.europa.eu/competition/elojade/isef/case_de-tails.cfm?proc_code=3_SA_38373 (accessed 4 March 2017).

118. EU Commission, 'State Aid: Ireland Gave Illegal Tax Benefits to Apple Worth up to €13 billion', (30 August 2016) http:// europa.eu/rapid/press-release_IP-16-2923_en.htm (accessed 28 February 2017).

119. Ibid.

120. 'Apple Tax Case: Why is Ireland Refusing Billions?' BBC News (7 September 2016), http://www.bbc.bom/news/world-europe-37299430 (accessed 28 February 2017).

121. Department of Finance, 'Minister Noonan Disagrees Profoundly with Commission on Apple' (30 August 2016). http://www.finance.gov.ie/news-centre/press-releases/minister-noonan-disagrees-profoundly-commission-apple (accessed 4 March 2017).

122. Ibid.

123. AFP, 'Apple to Fight Record EU Tax Bill' (31 August 2016). https://www.yahoo.com/news/apple-faces-huge-irish-tax-payout-eu-case-090854942.html (accessed 4 March 2017).

124. Permanent Subcommittee on Investigations, *Offshore Profit Shifting and the U.S. Tax Code – Part 2 (Apple Inc)*, 21 May 2013. https://www.hsgac.senate.gov/subcommittees/investigations/hearings/offshore-profit-shifting-and-the-us-tax-code_-part-2 (accessed 6 August 2016).

125. Ibid., p. 5.

126. Ibid., p. 78.

127. Wolfgang Schön, 'Tax Legislation and the Notion of Fiscal Aid: A Review of 5 Years of European Jurisprudence', in Isabelle Richelle, Wolfgang Schön and Edoardo Traversa (eds), *State Aid Law and Business Taxation: MPI Studies in Tax Law and Public Finance 6* (Heidelberg: Springer, 2016), p. 7.

128. Case C-387/92 (Banco Exterior de España) judgement of 15 March 1994, paragraph 14.

129. 'According to the case law of the Union Courts, the notion of aid embraces not only positive benefits, but also measures which, in various forms, mitigate the charges which are normally included in the budget of an undertaking. Although a measure that entails a reduction to a tax or a levy does not involve a positive transfer of resources from the State, it gives rise to an advantage because it places the undertakings to which it applies in a more favourable financial position than other taxpayers

and results in a loss of income to the State.' Case C/2016/4056 (Hungary) judgement of 4 July 2016, paragraph 12.

130. Department of Finance, *Explanatory Memorandum for the Information of Members of the Oireachtas: Dáil Debate of Government Motion on the Apple State Aid Case* (7 September 2016: 13). https://static.rasset.ie/documents/business/160906-explan-me-mo-for-info-of-memb-of-oireachtas-on-apple-case.pdf (accessed 5 March 2017).

131. Government Appeal of European Commission Decision on State Aid to Apple: Motion. Dáil Éireann, 7 September 2016. All subsequent quotes from this debate from this source.

132. Stephen Collins, *Irish Times* Poll: Majority Support Appeal of Apple Ruling', *Irish Times*, 10 October 2016. Of those polled 47 per cent supported the government's appeal, 39 per cent did not.

133. Brian Keegan, 'Tax Take', *Sunday Business Post*, 28 August 2016.

134. Dáil Éireann, Written Answers, 22 June 2016: 17575/16.

135. 'The Tax Justice Network is an independent international network launched in 2003. We are dedicated to high-level research, analysis and advocacy in the area of international tax and the international aspects of financial regulation. We map, analyse and explain the role of tax and the harmful impacts of tax evasion, tax avoidance, tax competition and tax havens. The world of offshore tax havens is a particular focus of our work. Our core goals are to create understanding and debate and to promote reform, especially in poorer countries. We are not aligned to any political party.' https://www.taxjustice.net/about/who-we-are/ (accessed 6 January 2018).

136. James S. Henry, 'The Price of Offshore Revisited', *Tax Justice Network* (July 2012), p. 5.

137. Anon., 'Banking Commission's Recommendations', *Irish Times*, 22 January 1927.

138. The story shows up in the 1996 movie *Michael Collins*, written and directed by Neil Jordon. Eileen Battersby also

recounts it in her article, 'Through the Past Darkly', *Irish Times*, 19 March 2005.

139. Conor McNamara, 'A Tenant's League or a Shopkeepers' League? Urban Protest and the Town Tenants' Association in the West of Ireland, 1909–1918', *Studia Hibernica*, no. 36 (2009–10), p. 158. For more on the ranch wars see Tony Varley, 'A Region of Sturdy Smallholders? Western Nationalists and Agrarian Politics during the First World War', *Journal of the Galway Archaeological and Historical Society*, vol. 55 (2003), pp. 127–55; Fergus Campbell, *Land and Revolution: Politics in the West of Ireland, 1898–1921* (Oxford: Oxford University Press, 2005), pp. 85–166.

140. Paul Rouse, *Ireland's Own Soil: Government and Agriculture in Ireland, 1945 to 1965* (Dublin: Irish Farmers Journal, 2000), p. 9.

141. Mary E. Daly, *Industrial Development and Irish National Identity, 1922–1939* (New York, 1992), p. 16.

142. Ronan Fanning, *The Irish Department of Finance, 1922–58* (Dublin: Institute of Public Administration, 1978), p. 99.

143. Joe Lee, *Ireland 1912–1985: Politics and Society* (Cambridge: Cambridge University Press, 1990), p. 108.

144. Anon., 'Bank of Ireland: Free State's Financial Agents', *Irish Times*, 21 January 1922.

145. Ibid.

146. Ibid.

147. Anon., 'Banking Commission's Recommendations'.

148. Ibid.

149. Ibid.

150. Anon., 'A Great Wall of Tariffs', *Irish Times*, 12 January 1929.

151. Eoin Drea, 'The Role of T.A. Smiddy in Fianna Fáil Economic Policy-making 1932–45', *Irish Studies Review*, vol. 24, no. 2 (2016), p. 179. Merrion Street is the address of the Department of Finance.

152. Maurice Moynihan, *Currency and Central Banking in Ireland, 1922–60* (Dublin: Gill & Macmillan, 1975), p. 286.

153. Currency Commission, *Report of the Currency Commission for the Year Ended 31ˢᵗ March 1935* (Dublin: Stationery Office, 1935), p. 7.

154. *Commission of Inquiry into Banking, Currency and Credit, 1938* (Dublin: Stationery Office, 1938), p. 578.

155. Ibid., p. 579.

156. Ibid., p. 584.

157. Ibid., p. 585.

158. Ibid.

159. Moynihan, *Currency and Central* Banking, p. 310.

160. The sterling area included Britain's colonies as well as Burma, Iceland, Ireland, Jordan, Libya, the Persian Gulf Territories and all Commonwealth countries with the exception of Canada.

161. From an article by Jack White, who was the London editor of *The Irish Times*.

162. Michael J. Hogan, *The Marshall Plan: America, Britain, and the Reconstruction of Western Europe, 1947–1952* (Cambridge: Cambridge University Press, 2002), p. 19.

163. Leo Panitch and Sam Gindin, *The Making of Global Capitalism: The Political Economy of the American Empire* (London: Verso, 2013), p. 95.

164. From 1947 to 1957 Ireland received £46.7m under the scheme, of which only £6.1m consisted of grants. See Bernadette Whelan, 'The New World and the Old: American Marshall Planners in Ireland, 1947–57, *Irish Studies in International Affairs*, vol. 12 (2001), p. 80.

165. Department of External Affairs, *The European Recovery Programme: Ireland's Long-Term Programme (1949–1953)* (Dublin: Stationery Office, 1948), p. 133.

166. Ibid.

167. Central Bank of Ireland, *Report of the Central Bank of Ireland for the Year Ended 31ˢᵗ March 1947* (Dublin: Stationery Office, 1947), p. 11.

168. Ibid.

169. Department of External Affairs, *European Recovery Programme*, p. 134.

170. Ibid. The OEEC is today the OECD.

171. Department of External Affairs, *European Recovery Programme*, p. xix.

172. For more on this see C. McCabe, *Sins of the Father: The Decisions that Shaped the Irish Economy*, 2nd edn (Dublin: History Press Ireland, 2013), pp. 96–174.

173. Anon., 'FF Outlines Plan to Financial Services Companies', *Irish Times*, 14 February 1987.

174. Anon., 'Leasing: The Rush for the Docks', *Finance* (April 1988), p. 9.

175. Anon., 'IFSC Goes Critical', *Finance* (June 1991), p. 5.

176. Kevin Warren, 'Tax Practice in the 1990s', *Finance* (July 1991), p. 13.

177. Anon., 'Germany and the IFSC', *Finance* (September 1991), p. 25.

178. John Stanley, 'The German Domino', *Finance* (October 1991), p. 4.

179. Dermot Desmond, 'Ireland's Edge: Tax Breaks and Minimal Rules', *Irish Times*, 31 October 1990.

180. Dermot Desmond, 'Financial Services See Huge Changes', *Irish Times*,
30 December 1987.

181. Brian Geegan, '1992 Regulation Offers IFSC Competitive Advantage', *Irish Times*, 14 February 1990.

182. Anon., 'IFSC Tax Deadline To Be Extended', *Irish Times*, 14 May 1990.

183. Joseph McArdle, 'The IFSC', *Finance* (February 1992), p. 12.

184. Steve Lohr, 'Offshore Banking's Umbrella Shields More than B.C.C.I.', *New York Times*, 11 August 1991.

185. Brian Lavery and Timothy O'Brien, 'For Insurance Regulators, Trails Lead to Dublin', *New York Times*, 1 April 2005.

186. Editorial, 'Policing the Financial Sector', *Irish Times*, 25 August 2007.

187. Joint Committee of Inquiry into the Banking Crisis Debate, Wednesday, 28 January 2015: Professor Ed Kane. https://beta.oireachtas.ie/en/debates/debate/joint_committee_of_inquiry_into_the_banking_crisis/2015-01-28/2/#s3 (accessed 10 January 2018).

188. 'Another piece of the financial system is the set of financial intermediaries through which households can indirectly provide resources for investment. As the term suggests, a financial intermediary stands between the two sides of the market and helps move financial resources toward their best use. Commercial banks are the best-known type of financial intermediary. They take deposits from savers and use these deposits to make loans to those who have investment projects they need to finance. Other examples of financial intermediaries include mutual funds, pension funds, and insurance companies. When an intermediary is involved, the financing is considered indirect because the saver is often unaware of whose investments his funds are financing.' Mankiw, *Macroeconomics*, p. 583.

189. Michael McLeay, Amar Radia and Ryland Thomas, 'Money Creation in the Modern Economy', *Bank of England Quarterly Bulletin* (2014 Q1), p. 1.

190. Conor McCabe, *Sins of the Father: The Decisions that Shaped the Irish Economy*, 2nd edn (Dublin: History Press Ireland, 2013), pp. 175–244.

191. Brendan McDonagh, 'Opening Statement by Mr. Brendan McDonagh, Chief Executive of NAMA, Joint Committee of Inquiry into the Banking Crisis, Wednesday, 22 April 2015', p. 11. https://www.nama.ie/fileadmin/user_upload/Brendan McDonagh_NAMACEO_OpeningAddress_BankingInquiry.pdf (accessed 10 January 2017).

192. Ibid., p. 12.

193. *Prime Time*, 24 November 2010. http://youtube.com/watch?v=YK7w6fXoYxo (accessed 23 Jul 2013).

194. *Commission Decision N725/2009: Irish Asset Relief – NAMA* (26 Feb. 2010), p. 4. http://ec.europa.eu/competition/elojade/isef/case_details.cfm?proc_code=3_n725_2009 (accessed 23 July 2013).

195. Parliamentary Question no. 91 to the Minister for Finance, 21 March 2013. http://oireachtasdebates.oireachtas.ie/debates%20authoring/debateswebpack.nsf/takes/dail2013032100054?opendocument#WRH01650 (accessed 24 July 2013).

196. Karl Whelan, *The ECB's Role in Financial Assistance Programmes* (Brussels: European Union, 2012), p. 5.

197. *Dáil Debates*, 4 November 2009, vol. 693, no. 2, paragraph 619.

198. Senan Moloney, 'Failed Bank Got All Clear in €7.4m Report', *Irish Independent*, 5 November 2009.

199. Morgan Kelly, 'Piling Anglo Losses on to National Debt Risks Bankrupting the State,' *Irish Times*, 20 January 2009.

200. Brian Lenihan Jr, 'An Opportunity for Us all to Pull Together and play our part', *Irish Times*, 15 October 2008. Subsequent quotes from the minister's speech are taken from this source.

201. Jonathan Kirshner, 'The Inescapable Politics of Money', in Jonathan Kirshner (ed.), *Monetary Orders: Ambiguous Economics, Ubiquitous Politics* (Ithaca: Cornell University Press, 2003), p. 3.

202. Mies and Bennholdt-Thomsen, *The Subsistence Perspective*, p. 5.

203. Geoff Mann, *Disassembly Required: A Field Guide to Actually Existing Capitalism* (Edinburgh: AK Press, 2013), p. 8.

204. See Ingham, *Capitalism*, pp. 52–62.

205. Mann, *Disassembly Required*, p. 2.

206. Fintan O'Toole, *Ship of Fools: How Stupidity and Corruption Sank the Celtic Tiger* (London: Faber & Faber, 2009), p. 71.

207. Ibid., p. 22.

208. Arthur Beesley, 'IL&P Deluding Itself with Talk of Integrity', *Irish Times*, 14 February 2009.

209. Alan Aherne, 'The Immorality and Unfairness of NAMA', *Irish Times*, 7 September 2009.

210. Gordon Brown, *Beyond the Crash: Overcoming the First Crisis of Globalisation* (London: Simon & Schuster, 2011), p. 241. Brown of course spent his time in government cutting the rule book and facilitating the type of self-regulating environment that finance demanded. He currently serves as an adviser to PIMCO, the vulture fund investment corporation which is in the process of evicting thousands of families from their houses via its wholly owned company, Havenbrook. He donates his fee to charity, presumably to bring balance to his morality karma.

211. Committee on Oversight and Government Reform, 'Hearings into the Financial Crisis and the Role of Financial Regulators', 23 October 2008 (serial no. 110-209). https://www.gpo.gov/fdsys/pkg/CHRG-110hhrg55764/html/CHRG-110hhrg55764.htm (accessed 21 June 2017).

212. Willem Buiter, 'The Unfortunate Uselessness of Most 'State of the Art' Academic Monetary Economics', MPRA Paper No. 58407 (2009): 1. https://mpra.ub.uni-muenchen.de/58407/1/MPRA_paper_58407.pdf (accessed 23 June 2017). All subsequent quotes from Buiter are from this source.

213. Stanford, *Economics for Everyone*, p. 1.

214. 'Once we admit that institutions are man-made and at least in part the product of conscious decision, we must also face the effects of institutional arrangements on social results.' Hyman Minsky, *Stabilizing an Unstable Economy* (New York: McGraw Hill, 1986), p. 9.

215. Stanford, *Economics for Everyone*, p. 3.

216. Michael Perelman, *Railroading Economics* (New York: Monthly Review Press, 2006), p. 17.

217. Thomas Piketty, *Capital in the Twenty-first Century* (Cambridge, MA: Harvard University Press, 2014), p. 20.

218. Ibid.

219. Ibid., p. 21.

220. Ibid., p. 471.

221. Ibid.

222. Ibid., p. 480.

223. Ibid., p. 479.

224. Ibid.

225. Joseph E. Stiglitz, *Rewriting the Rules of the American Economy: An Agenda for Growth and Shared Prosperity* (New York: Roosevelt Institute, 2015), p. 15.

226. Ibid., p. 12.

227. Ibid.

228. Ibid.

229. Ibid., p. 7.

230. Ibid.

231. Quoted in A. Shawki, *Black Liberation and Socialism* (Chicago: Haymarket Books, 2006), p. 13.

232. Karl Marx, *Capital: A Critique of Political Economy*, vol. 1 (London: Penguin Books, 1990), p. 344.

233. David Harvey, *The Condition of Postmodernity* (Cambridge, MA: Blackwell, 1989), p. 173.

234. Ibid.

235. Asbjørn Wahl, *The Rise and Fall of the Welfare State* (London: Pluto Press, 2011), p. 18.

236. Ibid.

237. Dexter Whitfield, *In Place of Austerity: Restructuring the Economy, State and Public Services* (Nottingham: Spokesman, 2012), p. 4.

238. Ibid., p. 116

239. Ibid., pp. 1–2.

240. Ian Harnett and David Bowers, 'Days of Inflation Targeting Are Numbered', *Financial Times*, 8 April 2013.

241. Ibid.

242. Harry G. Johnson, 'Problems of Efficiency in Monetary Management', *Journal of Political Economy*, vol. 76, no. 5 (Sep–Oct 1968), p. 986.

243. Ben Stein, 'In Class Warfare, Guess Which Class Is Winning', *New York Times*, 26 November 2006.

244. Wahl, *The Rise and Fall of the Welfare State*, p. 180.

245. Whitfield, *In Place of Austerity*, p. 117.

246. Dan Clawson, *The Next Upsurge: Labor and the New Social Movements* (Ithaca: Cornell University Press, 2003), p. 195.

247. Mies and Bennholdt-Thomsen, *The Subsistence Perspective*, p. 11.

248. Anon., 'International Feminism', *Off Our Backs* (Feb–Mar 1973),
p. 8. All subsequent quotes relating to this statement are from this source.

249. Mariarosa Dalla Costa and Selma James, 'The Power of Women and the Subversion of the Community', in Ellen Malos (ed.), *The Politics of Housework* (London: Allison & Busby, 1980), p. 162.

250. Ibid.

251. Pat Armstrong and Hugh Armstrong, 'Beyond Sexless Class and Classless Sex: Towards Feminist Marxism', *Studies in Political Economy*, vol. 10 (1983), p. 18.

252. Eric Olin Wright, 'Transforming Capitalism through Real Utopias', *American Sociological Review*, vol. 78, no. 1 (February 2013), p. 8.

253. Feminist Fightback, 'Cuts Are a Feminist Issue', *Soundings* vol. 49 (2011), p. 73.

254. Ibid., p. 75.

255. Ibid., p. 79.

256. A cryptocurrency (or crypto currency) is a digital asset designed to work as a currency that uses cryptography to secure its transactions; local exchange trading systems (LETS) are ones where members exchange goods and services by using locally created currency.

257. Trace Alloway, 'Virtual Money, from Real Central Bank Mistrust', *Financial Times*, 6 June 2011.

258. '... each Bitcoin user downloads and runs a P2P client program on their PC that communicates with similar programs being run by other users. Then a lottery ensues: the software on each P2P client runs a mathematical routine that attempts to generate a number lower than a constantly changing target figure ... one client succeeds and is rewarded with a certain amount of virtual money ... Because striking lucky this way is seen as akin to prospecting for gold, users have been dubbed "miners".' 'Virtual Money Gets Real', *New Scientist*, 4 June 2011, vol. 210, no. 2815, p. 23.

259. Ibid.

260. Minsky, *Stabilizing an Unstable Economy*, p. 1.

261. For more on this see Conor McCabe, *Sins of the Father: The Decisions that Shaped the Irish Economy* (Dublin: History Press Ireland, 2013), pp. 9–60.

262. This is based on an old Yiddish phrase, *der mentsh trakht un got lakht*.

263. Éric Tymoigne and L. Randall Wray, 'Money: An Alternative Story', in Philip Arestis and Malcolm Sawyer (eds) *A Handbook of Alternative Monetary Economics* (Cheltenham: Edward Elgar, 2006), p. 1. ashx?command=getcontent&server=webdocs& value=%5CBWC%5CBWC595-01.pdf (accessed 18 August 2012).

Bibliography

OFFICIAL PUBLICATIONS

Central Bank of Ireland, *Report of the Central Bank of Ireland for the Year Ended 31st March 1947* (Dublin: Stationery Office, 1947)

Commission of Inquiry into Banking, Currency and Credit, *Reports* (Dublin: Stationery Office, 1938)

Committee on Oversight and Government Reform, *Hearings into the Financial Crisis and the Role of Financial Regulators*, 23 October 2008 (serial no. 110–209)

Currency Commission, *Report of the Currency Commission for the Year Ended 31st March 1935* (Dublin: Stationery Office, 1935)

Department of External Affairs, *The European Recovery Programme: Ireland's Long-Term Programme (1949–1953)* (Dublin: Stationery Office, 1948)

Department of Finance, *Explanatory Memorandum for the Information of Members of the Oireachtas: Dáil Debate of Government Motion on the Apple State Aid Case, 7 September 2016* (2016)

EU Commission, Commission *Decision of 30.8.2016 on State Aid Sa.38373 (2014/C) (Ex 2014/Nn) (Ex 2014/Cp) Implemented by Ireland to Apple C(2016) 5605* (Brussels: EU Commission, 2016)

Financial Crisis Inquiry Commission, *The Financial Crisis Inquiry Report* (New York: Public Affairs, 2011)

Joint Committee of Inquiry into the Banking Crisis, *Report, Volumes 1–3* (Dublin: Stationery Office, 2016)

United Nations Monetary and Financial Conference, *Bretton Woods, New Hampshire, July 1 to July 22, 1944, Final Act and Related Documents* (Washington: US Printing Office, 1944)

United States Permanent Subcommittee on Investigations, *Repatriating Offshore Funds: 2004 Tax Windfall for Select Multinationals–Majority Staff Report* (October 2011)

United States Permanent Subcommittee on Investigations, *Offshore Profit Shifting and the US Tax Code – Part 2 (Apple Inc)*, 21 May 2013

BOOKS AND ARTICLES

Andrews, David M., 'Bretton Woods: System and Order,' in David M. Andrews (ed.), *Orderly Change: International Monetary Relations Since Bretton Woods* (Ithaca: Cornell University Press, 2008)

Armstrong, Pat, and Hugh Armstrong, 'Beyond Sexless Class and Classless Sex: Towards Feminist Marxism', *Studies in Political Economy*, vol. 10 (1983)

Arrighi, Giovanni, *The Long Twentieth Century: Money, Power and the Origins of Our Times*, 2nd edn (London: Verso, 2010)

Beresiner, Yasha and C.C. Narbeth, *The Story of Paper Money* (Bath: Pitman Press, 1973)

Braudel, Fernand, *Civilisation and Capitalism, 15th–18th Century, Vol. 1: The Structures of Everyday Life* (London: Fontana Press, 1985)

Braudel, Fernand, *Civilization and Capitalism, 15th–18th Century, Vol. 2: The Wheels of Commerce* (London: Collins, 1982)

Brown, Gordon, *Beyond the Crash: Overcoming the First Crisis of Globalisation* (London: Simon & Schuster, 2011)

Buiter, Willem, 'The Unfortunate Uselessness of Most "State of the Art" Academic Monetary Economics', *MPRA* Paper No. 58407 (2009)

Caliara, Aldo, Sally-Anne Way, Natalie Raaber, Anne Schoenstein, Radhika Balakrishan and Nicholas Lusiani, *Bringing Human Rights to Bear in Times of Crisis* (New York: ESCR-Net, 2010)

Campbell, Fergus, *Land and Revolution: Politics in the West of Ireland, 1898–1921* (Oxford: Oxford University Press, 2005)

Child, Josiah, *A Discourse of the Nature, Use and Advantage of Trade* (London, 1694)

Clawson, Dan, *The Next Upsurge: Labor and the New Social Movements* (Ithaca: Cornell University Press, 2003)

Dalla Costa, Mariarosa and Selma James, 'The Power of Women and the Subversion of the Community', in Ellen Malos (ed.), *The Politics of Housework* (London: Allison & Busby, 1980)

Daly, Mary E., *Industrial Development and Irish National Identity, 1922–1939* (New York: Syracuse University Press, 1992)

Desan, Christine, 'Coin Reconsidered: The Political Alchemy of Commodity Money', *Theoretical Inquiries in Law*, vol. 11, no. 1 (2010)

Desan, Christine, *Making Money: Coin, Currency, and the Coming of Capitalism* (Oxford: Oxford University Press, 2014)

Drea, Eoin, 'The Role of T.A. Smiddy in Fianna Fáil Economic Policy-making, 1932–45', *Irish Studies Review*, vol. 24, no. 2 (2016)

Eagleton, Catherine and Jonathan Williams, *Money: A History*, 2nd edn (London: British Museum Press, 2007)

Eatwell John, and Lance Taylor, *Global Finance at Risk: The Case for International Regulation* (Cambridge: Polity Press, 2000)

Einzig, Paul, 'Statics and Dynamics of the Euro-dollar Market', *The Economic Journal*, vol. 71, no. 283 (September 1961)

Epstein, Gerald A., 'Introduction: Financialization and the World Economy' in Gerald A. Epstein (ed.), *Financialization and the World Economy* (Cheltenham: Edward Elgar, 2005)

Fanning, Ronan, *The Irish Department of Finance, 1922–58* (Dublin: Institute of Public Administration, 1978)

Federici, Silvia, *Caliban and the Witch* (Brooklyn: Autonomedia, 2004)

Feminist Fightback, 'Cuts Are a Feminist Issue', *Soundings*, vol. 49 (2011)

Fontanel, Jacques, Jean-Paul Hebert and Ivan Samson, 'The Birth of the Political Economy or the Economy in the Heart of Politics: Mercantilism', *Defence and Peace Economics*, vol. 19, no. 5 (2008)

Garfinkle, Steven J., 'Shepherds, Merchants, and Credit: Some Observations on Lending Practices in Ur III Mesopotamia', *Journal of the Economic and Social History of the Orient*, vol. 47, no. 1 (2004)

Gerriets, Marilyn, 'Money in Early Christian Ireland According to the Irish Laws', *Comparative Studies in Society and History*, vol. 27, no. 2 (1985)

Graeber, David, *Debt: The First 5,000 Years* (Brooklyn: Melville House Publishing, 2011)

Haley, K.H.D., *The Dutch in the Seventeenth Century* (London: Thames & Hudson, 1972)

Harvey, David, *A Brief History of Neoliberalism* (Oxford: Oxford University Press, 2007)

Harvey, David, *The Condition of Postmodernity* (Cambridge, MA: Blackwell, 1989)

Helleiner, Eric, 'From Bretton Woods to Global Finance: A World Turned Upside Down', in Richard Stubbs and Geoffrey R.D. Underhill (eds), *Political Economy and the Changing Global Order* (London: Macmillan, 1994)

Helleiner, Eric, *States and the Reemergence of Global Finance: From Bretton Woods to the 1990s* (Ithaca: Cornell University Press, 1996)

Henry, James, 'The Price of Offshore Revisited', *Tax Justice Network* (July 2012)

Hewson, John and Eisuke Sakakibara, *The Eurocurrency Markets and Their Implications: A New View of International Monetary Problems and Monetary Reform* (Lexington: Lexington Books, 1975)

Hogan, Michael J., *The Marshall Plan: America, Britain, and the Reconstruction of Western Europe, 1947–1952* (Cambridge: Cambridge University Press, 1987)

Horton, Myles and P. Freire, *We Make the Road by Walking* (Philadelphia: Temple University Press, 1990)

Humphrey, Caroline, 'Barter and Economic Disintegration', *Man*, vol. 20, no. 1 (March 1985)

Ingham, Geoffrey, *The Nature of Money* (Cambridge: Polity Press, 2004)

Ingham, Geoffrey, *Capitalism* (Cambridge: Polity Press, 2008)

International Federation for Human Rights, *Downgrading Rights: The Cost of Austerity in Greece* (Athens: FIDH, 2014)

Jevons, William Stanley, *Money and the Medium of Exchange* (New York: D. Appleton & Co., 1875)

Johnson, Harry G., 'Problems of Efficiency in Monetary Management', *Journal of Political Economy*, vol. 76, no. 5 (Sep–Oct 1968)

Jones, Philip, *The Italian City-State from Commune to Signoria* (Oxford: Clarendon Press, 1997)

Kindleberger, Charles P., *A Financial History of Western Europe* (London: George Allen & Unwin, 1984)

Kirshner, Jonathan, 'The Inescapable Politics of Money', in Jonathan Kirshner (ed.), *Monetary Orders: Ambiguous Economics, Ubiquitous Politics* (Ithaca: Cornell University Press, 2003)

Kripper, Greta, 'The Financialization of the American Economy', *Socio-Economic Review*, vol. 3, no. 2 (2005)

Law, John, *Essay on a Land Bank* (London, 1705)

Lee, Joe, *Ireland 1912–1985: Politics and Society* (Cambridge: Cambridge University Press, 1990)

Mankiw, N.G., *Macroeconomics*, 9th edn (New York: Worth Publishers, 2016)

Mann, Geoff, *In the Long Run: Keynesianism, Political Economy and Revolution* (London: Verso, 2017)

Mann, Geoff, *Disassembly Required: A Field Guide to Actually Existing Capitalism* (Edinburgh: AK Press, 2013)

Marx, Karl, *Capital: A Critique of Political Economy*, vol. 1 (London: Penguin, 1976)

Maxwell, Henry, *Mr. Maxwell's Second Letter to Mr. Romley; Wherein the Objections against the Bank Are Answered* (Dublin, 1721)

McCabe, Conor, *Sins of the Father: The Decisions that Shaped the Irish Economy*, 2nd edn (Dublin: History Press Ireland, 2013)

McLeay, Michael, Amar Radia and Ryland Thomas, 'Money Creation in the Modern Economy', *Bank of England Quarterly Bulletin* (2014)

McNamara, Conor, 'A Tenants' League or a Shopkeepers' League? Urban Protest and the Town Tenants' Association in the West of Ireland, 1909–1918', *Studia Hibernica*, no. 36 (2009–2010)

Mies, Maria and Veronika Bennholdt-Thomsen, *The Subsistence Perspective* (London: Zed Books, 1999)

Minsky, Hyman, *Stabilizing an Unstable Economy* (New York: McGraw Hill, 1986)

Moffitt, Michael, *The World's Money: From Bretton Woods to the Brink of Insolvency* (New York: Simon & Schuster, 1983)

Moynihan, Maurice, *Currency and Central Banking in Ireland, 1922–60* (Dublin: Gill & Macmillan, 1975)

O'Toole, Fintan, *Ship of Fools: How Stupidity and Corruption Sank the Celtic Tiger* (London: Faber & Faber, 2009)

Palan, Ronen, Richard Murphy and Christian Chavagneux, *Tax Havens: How Globalization Really Works* (Ithaca: Cornell University Press, 2010)

Panitch, Leo and Sam Gindin, *The Making of Global Capitalism: The Political Economy of the American Empire* (London: Verso, 2013)

Perelman, Michael, *Railroading Economics* (New York: Monthly Review Press, 2006)

Piketty, Thomas, *Capital in the Twenty-first Century* (Cambridge, MA: Harvard University Press, 2014)

Pincus, Stephen, 'A Revolution in Political Economy?' in Maximillian E. Novak (ed.), *The Age of Projects* (Toronto: University of Toronto Press, 2008)

Polo, Marco, *The Travels of Marco Polo* (Edinburgh: Oliver & Boyd, 1845)

Reynell, Carew, *The True English Interest* (London, 1674)

Roth, Martha T., *Law Collections from Mesopotamia and Asia Minor*, 2nd edn (Atlanta: Scholars Press, 1997)

Rouse, Paul, *Ireland's Own Soil: Government and Agriculture in Ireland, 1945 to 1965* (Dublin: Irish Farmers Journal, 2000)

Schön, Wolfgang, 'Tax Legislation and the Notion of Fiscal Aid: A Review of 5 Years of European Jurisprudence, in Isabelle Richelle, Wolfgang Schön and Edoardo Traversa (eds), *State Aid Law and Business Taxation: MPI Studies in Tax Law and Public Finance*, vol. 6 (Heidelberg: Springer, 2016)

Schumpeter, Joseph, *History of Economic Analysis* (New York: Oxford University Press, 1954)

Shawki, Ahmed, *Black Liberation and Socialism* (Chicago: Haymarket Books, 2006)

Spufford, Peter, *Money and Its Use in Medieval Europe* (Cambridge: Cambridge University Press, 1988)

Stanford, Jim, *Economics for Everyone: A Short Guide to the Economics of Capitalism* (London: Pluto Press, 2008)

Steil, Benn, *The Battle of Bretton Woods: John Maynard Keynes, Harry Dexter White, and the Making of a New World Order* (Princeton: Princeton University Press, 2014)

Stiglitz, Joseph E., *Rewriting the Rules of the American Economy: An Agenda for Growth and Shared Prosperity* (New York: Roosevelt Institute, 2015)

Tabb, William K., *The Long Default: New York City and the Urban Fiscal Crisis* (New York: Monthly Review Press, 1982)

Tymoigne, Éric and L. Randall Wray, 'Money: An Alternative Story' in Philip Arestis and Malcolm Sawyer (eds), *A Handbook of Alternative Monetary Economics* (Cheltenham: Edward Elgar, 2006)

Varley, Tony, 'A Region of Sturdy Smallholders? Western Nationalists and Agrarian Politics during the First World War', *Journal of the Galway Archaeological and Historical Society*, vol. 55 (2003)

Wahl, Asbjørn, *The Rise and Fall of the Welfare State* (London: Pluto Press, 2011)

Wallerstein, Immanuel, *Historical Capitalism* (London: Verso, 1983)

Werner, Richard, *Princes of the Yen: Japan's Central Bankers and the Transformation of the Economy* (London: Routledge, 2003)

Whelan, Bernadette, 'The New World and the Old: American Marshall Planners in Ireland, 1947–57', *Irish Studies in International Affairs*, vol. 12 (2001)

Whelan, Karl, *The ECB's Role in Financial Assistance Programmes* (Brussels: European Union, 2012)

Whitfield, Dexter, *In Place of Austerity: Restructuring the Economy, State and Public Services* (Nottingham: Spokesman, 2012)

Wood, Ellen Meiksins, *The Origin of Capitalism: A Longer View* (London: Verso, 2002)

Wood, Ellen Meiksins, *Democracy Against Capitalism: Renewing Historical Materialism*, 2nd edn (London: Verso, 2016)

Wright, Eric Olin, 'Transforming Capitalism through Real Utopias', *American Sociological Review*, vol. 78, no. 1 (February 2011)

Index